THE STANLEY HOLLOWAY MONOLOGUES

Stanley Holloway, OBE, was born in 1890 and was originally a seaside concert artist. He first appeared on the London stage in 1919 and since then has performed in scores of straight plays, musical comedies, pantomimes, films and solo performances on both sides of the Atlantic. He will always be remembered as Alfred P. Doolittle in *My Fair Lady* as well as for his unparalleled rendering of the comic monologue. Mr Holloway now lives in Sussex, still making records and appearing on television from time to time.

This unique collection of the monologues marks the Fiftieth Anniversary of both the writing and the first performance of 'Sam, Pick Oop Tha' Musket', and brings together for the first time thirty-three other monologues written by, amongst others, Marriott Edgar, Bert Weston, Bob Lee, and Stanley Holloway himself. The monologues have been performed by Mr Holloway, in his own inimitable style, over the last half century and all the classics are included here, as well as a number of compositions which have never previously been published.

The monologues have been collected and are introduced by Michael Marshall, a theatrical and film historian, whose book *Top Hat & Tails* – the biography of Jack Buchanan – was published by Elm Tree Books in 1978. Mr Marshall has been the Member of Parliament for Arundel since 1974.

Also by Michael Marshall

TOP HAT AND TAILS

THE STANLEY HOLLOWAY MONOLOGUES

Edited and with an introduction by

MICHAEL MARSHALL

Illustrated by Bill Tidy

ELM TREE BOOKS/
EMI MUSIC PUBLISHING

To STANLEY HOLLOWAY –
a great artist who made all this possible

First published in Great Britain 1979
by Elm Tree Books/Hamish Hamilton Ltd
Garden House 57–59 Long Acre London WC2E 9JZ
in association with EMI Music Publishing Ltd
138–140 Charing Cross Road London Wc2H 0LD

Introduction copyright © 1979 by Michael Marshall
See also further copyright acknowledgements on page xix

British Library Cataloguing in Publication Data

The complete Holloway monologues.
  1. Humorous poetry, English
  2. Humorous recitations
  3. English poetry – 20th century
  I. Holloway, Stanley II. Marshall, Michael *b. 1930*
  821'.07   PR1195.H8

  ISBN 0–241–10306–1

Typeset and printed in Great Britain by
Lowe & Brydone Printers Ltd Thetford Norfolk

CONTENTS

Part IV: MONOLOGUE DISCOGRAPHY

FOREWORD

by Stanley Holloway

This is the first complete collection of the monologues almost all of which I originally performed between 1929 and 1941. Eleven of them have never been published before and the remaining twenty-three have never previously appeared in one volume.

Although I still know large parts of the monologues by heart, it was a new experience to read them – especially in the cases of Sam and Albert – as one continuous narrative. And even the Miscellaneous Section has a sort of logic which appeals to me in its history, humour and social comment.

Little did I think when I sat down to write the first monologue, Sam Small, that I was starting a kind of cult. This may sound rather grand from one who has always been proud to describe himself as an entertainer, but it gives me special pleasure to feel that the monologues have almost become part of the British way of life. In performing them, I tried to capture the spirit not only of Northerners like Sam Small and the Ramsbottoms, but also many of the virtues of all our Island race.

Perhaps it is that famous British ability to make fun of ourselves which is the most consistent theme in all the monologues. Certainly I was lucky that my writers Bob Weston and Bert Lee, Mabel Constanduras and Michael Hogan and, above all, 'George' Edgar could follow the pattern so faithfully which I established with Sam Small.

I have been lucky, too, in finding such a sympathetic spirit as Michael Marshall to bring all my old friends together again. We have spent many hours talking of the characters in the monologues; of my composers and the many places – often extremely unlikely – where these pieces were first conceived and performed. I hope reading them will give you as much pleasure as I have had in re-living them. And now, as the Duke said to Sam Small, 'Let battle commence.'

STANLEY HOLLOWAY

INTRODUCTION
by Michael Marshall

'Sam Small' made his first public appearance at the London Palladium in February 1929. The monologue in which he was introduced, 'Old Sam' ('Sam, Pick Oop Tha' Musket'), had been composed specially for the occasion by Stanley Holloway.

In 1929, Stanley Holloway was thirty-eight years old and best known as a rollicking baritone – a star for almost a decade of the concert party atmosphere of *The Co-Optimists*. His most famous songs were stirring numbers like 'The Cobbler', 'The Wheel-Tapper', and his then current hit, 'The Song of the Sea'. When he was invited to appear at the London Palladium, Stanley decided that something more than the usual baritone's selection was required. As so often in his life, it was his close friend, the brilliant, frog-faced comedian Leslie Henson who came up with an idea – an idea which was to begin the whole cult of the comedy monologue.

There had been monologuists a-plenty in the twentieth century and Stanley had already performed one semi-serious monologue, 'And Yet I don't Know', in Variety. Earlier he had studied the work of those who had performed before his time, like Corney Grain, Mel B. Spur and Bransby Williams whom he had seen many times on the Halls. However they had specialized in dramatic recitations; what Stanley had in mind now was a new approach – that of the broad comedy monologue. When it came to comedy, there was no one who was more expert than Leslie Henson. He had 'brought on' Stanley in West End revue and in musical comedy soon after the First World War and his suggestion for the Palladium appearance fired Stanley's imagination.

Leslie had read a book of Lancashire stories called *Cronies at the Inn* by Edwin J. Waugh and he mentioned one particular story to Stanley, *The King and the Volunteer*, in which a soldier accidentally drops his rifle. When he read this story himself Stanley Holloway recognized some promising material: he had always had a fertile mind and a facility for words. At his home in Hampstead one evening towards the end of 1928, he began to think about a character called Sam Small – a Yorkshire soldier. This was a logical choice as Stanley had served with a Yorkshire Regiment in the First World War and had acquired a close and detailed knowledge of Yorkshire dialect. He was also familiar with that confidential quality which he felt was a special feature of Northern humour, and which he recognized in *The King and the Volunteer* when the protagonists' friendship was described as 'After that, King and me got reet thick'.

Stanley went to bed with thoughts of Sam Small whirling in his mind. Unable to sleep, he got up and, writing on the backs of old envelopes, completed the first outline of 'Old Sam' in ten minutes. Recalling the event later, he said: 'It just flowed. It was as though I was writing a letter. I had to do some tidying up and minor corrections next day, but really the creation of "Old Sam" almost seemed to happen of its own accord.'

The Palladium audiences soon showed they loved the battle of wills between the stubborn Yorkshire character and the succession of superior officers who cannot persuade him to pick up his musket. Fifty years later, Stanley Holloway's television appearances and record re-issues show that audiences have a continuing zest for Sam's Yorkshire dialogue, and the neat four line verse with its rhyming pattern on the second and fourth lines which was to set the style for another ten Sam Small monologues.

''Alt! Who Goes There?'' was also written by Stanley Holloway when he was, as he says, in 'a sustained monologue mood'. It was composed while he was touring in *The Co-Optimists of 1930* and was released in the same year, together with 'Albert and The Lion', as the first Holloway monologue record.

In 'Beat the Retreat on Thy Drum' (1931), Stanley used the song-writing team of Bob Weston and Bert Lee, who had been responsible for the First World War hit 'Good-byee'. Bert Lee was a cheerful little Northerner who had started life as a piano tuner while Bob Weston, thick-set, short and inclined to deafness, was a Cockney. He was the ideas man and Bert Lee put in the tried and trusted gags. 'And Yet I Don't Know', which Stanley had used previously, was one of their monologue-songs. In 'Beat the Retreat' they showed instant skill in displaying the humourous Northern chauvinism so that Sam Small – even as a boy – is

'British and Yorkshire, ba goom'. This presented some translation difficulties when Stanley broadcast a French version for Kissproof Lipstick on Radio Paris.

Later in 1931, Stanley took up his own pen again to compose the self-explanatory tale of Sam's drinking downfall, 'One Each Apiece All Round'. The success of this and the earlier Sam sagas soon brought a positive rush of other Sam monologues composed by different writers, all remarkably faithful to the original concept.

First came the writing team of Mabel Constanduros and Michael Hogan with 'Sam's Medal' (1933). She was an actress as well as a writer and was soon to become famous as a radio performer in the role of 'Grandma Buggins'. Michael Hogan was a leading film-script writer. They were among the first to recognize the effectiveness of repeating certain key phrases and thus, when Sam goes to the Palace to be decorated, the Sentry, the Archbishop and the Prime Minister all tell him that the King has a medal for him. 'I know 'e 'as,' replies Sam. When he spoke these lines, Stanley Holloway made the very most of Sam's growing, 'no respecter of persons', exasperation. Mabel Constanduros was also responsible for 'Old Sam's Party' written as a Christmas record release in 1933. The published version is shorter than that used on the record which also worked in pieces from earlier monologues. 'Old Sam's Party' with its wide variety of guests who entertain the assembled company showed off Stanley Holloway's extraordinary range of voices, dialects and singing styles.

With 'Marksman Sam' (1934), Marriott Edgar made his first contribution to the Sam saga. As we shall see, he had earlier been responsible for creating the other great Holloway monologue character, Albert Ramsbottom. Marriott Edgar – always known as George – was a half brother to Edgar Wallace and, as his prodigious output shows, had much of the family's writing skills. Of medium height, he was a quiet man with a droll sense of humour and had worked as a performer in both concert party and pantomime including several spells with Stanley in the *Co-Optimists*. He was appearing in the *Fol-de-Rols* at Hastings when Stanley went to see him and one wet Saturday morning they began their collaboration on 'Marksman Sam'. This monologue is attributed to Marriott Edgar alone as Stanley valued him too much as a writer to argue over the author's credits. Certainly in this, as in all his compositions, Marriott Edgar showed an exceptional facility in idiom and rhyming. For example:

> Sam carried a musket, knapsack and coat
> Spur boots that 'e'd managed to wangle
> A 'atchet, a spade – in fact, as Sam said,
> 'E'd got everything bar t'kitchen mangle.

In 1935, Bob Weston and Bert Lee returned to the Sam theme in 'Sam Drummed Out'. By then, Stanley Holloway was coming under some pressure for his seeming Yorkshire preferences and this explains why – when Sam is restored as the pride of the regiment after 'a little local misunderstanding' – it has become the Lancashire 'Fuisilliers' (firmly mis-spelt to ensure strict observance of Lancashire dialect). With 'Sam's Sturgeon' (also written in 1935) a new composer's name appears – Ashley Sterne. For many years, this pen-name was a well-kept secret although keen devotees of *The Times* crossword puzzle might have solved the mystery. Today, it can be revealed that Ashley Sterne was an anagram of the name of the comic journalist Ernest Halsey – then writing for *London Opinion*.

During the Second World War, Marriott Edgar cheered everyone up with two final Sam contributions. 'Old Sam's Christmas Pudding' was recorded by Stanley Holloway in 1939. It is one of the best of George Edgar's compositions, yet limited wartime performing opportunities have made it relatively less known. Published here for the first time, the reader can readily imagine the relish with which Stanley Holloway revealed the true origin of the Fusiliers' (spelt correctly this time) cap badge and the marvellous double meaning he invested such lines as:

> The Spaniards had put up a bastion
> And ooh what a *bastion* it was.

In 'Sam Goes To It' (1941), Marriott Edgar used splendid poetic licence in bringing Sam Small – a veteran at Waterloo – out of his retirement as a volunteer 125 years later. But this allowed Stanley Holloway to perform a grand finale for Sam's military career and gave full effect to his impression of Winston Churchill interviewing what must have been 'Britain's oldest wartime recruit':

> 'I'll fit you in somewhere,' said Winnie,
> 'Old Soldiers we must not discard.'
> Then seeing he'd got his own musket,
> He sent him to join the Home Guard.

If Sam Small was Stanley Holloway's greatest original character – both as writer and performer – he was almost matched by his chief collaborator, Marriott Edgar. By 1932, George Edgar had been on several tours with Stanley in *The Co-Optimists* and other shows, and had studied the Sam monologues closely. A press report of a lion mauling a small boy at the London Zoo had caught his attention, but when George mentioned this as a possible plot, Stanley replied, 'Yes, I think it has possibilities but you'll have a hell of a job with that gruesome ending.' George Edgar however persevered and, by changing the venue to Blackpool, was able to inject the kind of Northern humour which is so often displayed in the face of personal tragedy. Nevertheless it was, Stanley Holloway now recalls, 'something of a gamble when we considered using "The Lion and Albert" for the Savoy Follies in 1932. So I decided to try out the number on one of my private cabaret appearances'.

Stanley was to use his monologues widely in cabaret at the Trocadero, The Piccadilly, Grosvenor House and Chez Henri in Long Acre. As he says today, 'I hated the work. It was what I called appearing before knives and forks!' Certainly the debut of 'The Lion and Albert' could not have been more challenging – the Northern Rugby League Annual Dinner and Dance at the Grand Hotel, Newcastle. Rugger dinners (even with dancing) are notorious as boisterous occasions but, as Stanley Holloway recalls:

> There was no platform because I was just appearing on the dancefloor. So I got an ordinary chair and stood on it to recite 'The Lion and Albert'. They were still finishing dinner with knives and forks clattering. But as I got to the end of the first verse, I found I was getting quiet all round. When it came to the lines. 'Took his stick with its 'orse's 'ead 'andle,/And pushed it in Wallace's ear,' it got a very big laugh. From that moment on, it was always a success, wherever I performed it.

George Edgar was soon hard at work on a sequel and 'The Return of Albert' was first performed in 1934. Before that, however, he found time to write 'Runcorn Ferry' (1933) in which Albert played a minor role in the clash of wills between his father and old Ted, the boatman, with their argument over 'Per Tuppence Per Person per Trip'. With these three 'Ramsbottom' tales, George Edgar's reputation as the greatest of all monologue writers was established and, in later years, he would perform many of the monologues himself. Although Stanley Holloway believes he was always a better creator than a performer, there is little doubt that they were able to work so well together since each understood the other's task from direct parallel experience.

The 'Ramsbottom' monologues continued in a steady stream. 'The Jubilee Sov'rin' and 'Albert and the 'Eadsman' were recorded in 1937 and 'The Recumbent Posture' in 1939. The first and third of these monologues, with their emphasis on Albert's stomach problems, always ensured that Stanley Holloway was a popular entertainer with the medical profession.

But Stanley was not content to remain solely a performer and in 1940 he wrote and recorded 'Albert Evacuated'. At about the same time, he also collaborated with the brilliant comedian Stanley Lupino to produce 'Albert's Reunion'.

The version of 'Albert's Reunion' on page 47 was rewritten by Stanley Holloway after the war and first recorded in the seventies; it provides a neat and happy ending to the Lion and Albert's exchanges. The 1978 date shown against this monologue reflects the continued durability and popularity of the Albert monologues and of their performer. In that year, at the age of eighty-eight, Stanley Holloway appeared on the BBC's 'Michael Parkinson Show'. He performed 'Albert and the Lion' and 'Albert's Reunion' with undiminished zest to prove, yet again, that 'Albert' will go on for ever.

So, too, will many of the historic characters in the fifteen 'Miscellaneous Monologues' which begin on page 51 They are almost equally divided between Stanley Holloway's principal contributors: seven are classic Marriott Edgar pieces and six are by Bob Weston and Bert Lee. These include a number of 'song-monologues' which Stanley used to vary the pattern of his performances. Variety was also the keynote in the two other 'Miscellaneous Monologues'.

'Many Happy Returns' (1933) was written by the former *Co-Optimist* publicity manager, Archie de Bear. It allowed Stanley to use his 'schoolmaster' voice and was, indeed, performed by him at several schools. Perhaps the most notable of these performances was at Stowe School in the mid-thirties. Stanley had met one of the Stowe masters on holiday who, after a convivial evening, had persuaded him to put on a cabaret at the school. They had agreed on a fee of twenty-five pounds and for this, in addition to his own performance of 'Many Happy

Returns', Stanley brought on as his supporting players Florence Desmond, Laddie Cliff and Billy Mayerl!

'The Parson of Puddle' (1938) was a song-monologue written by the concert party and revue specialist Rex Newman. For this Stanley used his 'clergyman' voice and, with its mild *double-entendres*, it was considered quite *risqué* at the time. The acknowledged masters of the song-monologue were, however, Bob Weston and Bert Lee. 'With Her Head Tucked Underneath Her Arm' (1934) is a prime example. It, too, was considered daring in referring to the 'Bloody' Tower. One of Stanley's earliest performances of the piece was for the BBC and there was a great debate with his producer before it was finally decided that the 'Bloody' Tower was an historic rather than an unparliamentary expression.

Weston and Lee's next contributions also developed historic themes in pure monologue form: 'The Beefeater' (1934) – again set at the Tower of London – and 'St George and The Dragon'. This was first performed by Stanley Holloway in 1935 but his recording of the monologue had to wait for another forty years; the original version is on page 64. For the 1975 LP Stanley re-wrote the ending so that 'Uncle' George's death is followed by the line 'Oh, I don't think he really deserved it'. To this Stanley added:

And that's the end of old George
And the end of the tale
And the tale – well
That's the end of the Dragon.

Weston and Lee's 'Brahn Boots' and 'Yorkshire Pudden' were first performed by Stanley in the thirties and recorded in 1940. 'Brahn Boots' is a real cockney song-monologue while 'Yorkshire Pudden' goes back to Northern dialect. The last Weston and Lee contribution in the Miscellaneous Section, 'Sweeney Todd, The Barber', is another song-monologue which Stanley had to wait for many years before recording in 1957. It is a rollicking tune which even the recent Sweeney Todd Broadway Musical cannot match.

Marriott Edgar's seven 'miscellaneous' monologues are, with one exception, all dead-pan comic contributions to history. 'Three Ha'pence a Foot (1932) gave a novel interpretation of Noah's haggling when preparing for the flood. Unlike the biblical texts, this flood started – where else? – in Lancashire and:

They said 'twas the rottenest summer
That Bury 'ad 'ad for some time.

The writing of 'Gunner Joe' (1933) was another example of mental telepathy in the Holloway/Edgar collaboration. Both were 'Brother Savages' – members of the famous theatrical club, The Savage, then at 1 Carlton House Terrace in London. One morning they were in their favourite working place – the Club's Billiard Room – discussing the lines which follow Nelson's decision to attack at Trafalgar. After 'They were in for a do it were plain', Stanley suggested, 'And Joe murmur'd shiver my timbers' and George Edgar, pacing up and down the billiard room, instantly replied, 'And Nelson kissed 'Ardy again'.

In 'The 'Ole in the Ark' (1937), George Edgar returned to his version of life at sea in Noah's ark. In the same year he developed another biblical sea-faring theme in 'Jonah and the Grampus'. Both these were conveniently produced at just the right moment to include them in one of the first television performances at Alexandra Palace. As Stanley recalls: 'They were very handy because camera movement was strictly limited in those early days and I could perform them in a static way concentrating on the voice and facial expressions.'

'Uppards' was written in the mid-thirties. It had a certain off-beat quality which surprised those who had become used to Marriott Edgar's historic themes. Perhaps for this reason it had less popular success than some of the earlier monologues, but Stanley Holloway always had a soft spot for this Lancashire version of 'Excelsior' and therefore chose it for a wartime revival with his recording in 1941. Similarly, 'The Battle of Hastings' and 'The Magna Charter' were two of Marriott Edgar's thirties compositions which Stanley recorded much later. Both were originally intended as material for Stanley's appearance at Drury Lane in the Kern–Hammerstein musical *Three Sisters* (1934).

When Hammerstein said he wanted his own songs in the show, George Edgar performed both monologues himself – it was over forty years later when Stanley first used them. Stanley derived particular satisfaction from the 1975 recordings for three reasons: first, because he had suggested the repeated use of ''Arold, on his 'orse with his 'awk in his 'and' in 'The Battle of Hastings'; second, because 'The Magna Charter' contained one of his favourite monologue endings and third, because if – as seems likely – these are his swansong recordings they went out under a title he relishes, 'Life in the Old Dog Yet'.

Those meeting Stanley Holloway today can confirm that the title still applies. Nowhere is this more evident than in his recollections of the monologues. In my many hours of conversation with him, he turned time and again to them – quoting long passages with all the vigour and attack of his first performances.

Some of the unpublished monologues presented special difficulties in tracing early and rare recordings. In the case of 'Many Happy Returns' by Archie de Bear (1933), the only record available in the BBC archives was partly broken and it was only possible to transcribe the second half. When told of this misfortune, Stanley said, 'Oh, that's no problem. Here we go', and promptly declaimed the first thirty-two lines as if he had been rehearsing the monologue for weeks. This extraordinary capacity for total recall is rare among artists but in Stanley's case there is little doubt that the monologues have become part of his own personal philosophy and the peculiar and special humour which has made him one of our greatest and best-loved English character actors.

He derives special pleasure from a feeling of shared inheritance in the monologues. Wherever he goes, he is greeted by those who are quick to identify themselves with them – so it has always been. It might be assumed that this would be a 'low-brow' group, but such is the brilliance of the material and the skill of the performer that their appeal is universal – even in the most exalted circles.

In the mid-thirties, Stanley attended Lady Wavertree's traditional pre-Wimbledon garden party. Suzanne Lenglen was there with the flyers, Jim and Amy Mollison. There were many other celebrities present – all anxious to meet Stanley. But the man who proved most determined to engage him in conversation was Prince George of Greece. Shaking Stanley by the hand, the Prince said, 'Oh, Mr Holloway, I've been dying to meet you – "It occurred on the evening before Waterloo, and troops were lined up on parade",' he went on, plunging rapidly into his version of 'Old Sam'.

In 1935, Gerald du Maurier arranged a cabaret at the Dorchester for George V's Diamond Jubilee. Among the audience were the Duke and Duchess of York (later George VI and Queen Elizabeth). Stanley came on to perform 'Albert and the Lion' and noticed that the Royal pair were listening to his performance with special care. When he came to the line 'A grand little lad was young Albert', the future Queen Mother gave

'Bertie', Duke of York, the most enormous dig in the ribs. Stanley prides himself that, in the following year, he steadfastly refused to perform an anonymous monologue entitled 'Edward and the Lioness'. This was an obvious skit on the abdication crisis making great play on Wallace the lion and Wallis, the future Duchess of Windsor. This piece was sent to Stanley from as far afield as India. Many whispered it was his own composition – a suggestion easily refuted by his refusal to perform it even on private occasions and the fact that – unlike amost all the other monologues – he canot recall a line of the original.

In post-war years, the Houses of Parliament have seemingly become a special repository of monologue expertise. While I was travelling to a speaking engagement with Sir Keith Joseph he demonstrated his mastery of the activities of both 'Sam' and 'Albert'. Recently Stanley Holloway at a charity ball was greeted in the middle of the dancefloor by Lord Robens who, revealing his Lancashire experience, and in particular his knowledge of 'Runcorn Ferry' said: 'T' transporter bridge is down!' More recently still, Stanley and his wife, Laney, found that Lord Robens's knowledge is widely shared in their Lordships' House. They were entertained to lunch in the House of Lords and their meal was interrupted by a steady stream of Peers coming up to be introduced and to quote the monologues on the basis of 'One Each Apiece All Round'.

The same story could be told of a large part of the British population. For, as Stanley says in his foreword, the monologues have become part of our way of life. But perhaps the appreciation he treasures most is that of his own peer group, the theatrical profession and one of their most enthusiastic voices is Laurence Olivier. In the twenties, as the son of a clergyman, he was often called on 'after supper' to perform some of the early Holloway songs like 'The Wheel-Tapper'. His appreciation of Stanley's work carried over into the monologue era of the thirties.

It was during this period that Stanley acquired one of his greatest and most perceptive admirers, the American dance director, Buddy Bradley. He summed up the true art of the Holloway monologues when he said: 'When I hear them, I don't laugh. I smile. They are made for chuckles not for belly laughs.' Buddy Bradley's comment sums up the full extent of Stanley Holloway's great monologue achievement. We remember them affectionately as old friends to whom we return again and again. When 'Sam Small' was first performed at the London Palladium in 1929, Stanley's co-stars included the stylish whistling comedian Albert Whelan. After hearing 'Sam, Pick Oop Tha' Musket', he said to Stanley, 'This is going to last you for years. You may tire of it but the audiences never will.'

Nor ever have we and, on this fiftieth anniversary, we salute the artist who has given us so much pleasure with the monologues which follow. Ladies and Gentlemen, it is my pleasure to introduce – the incomparable Stanley Holloway.

NOTES AND ACKNOWLEDGEMENTS

The thirty-four monologues in this book are those which are most closely associated with Stanley Holloway. The date shown against each in the Contents is that of his first recording, with the exception of 'Old Sam', 'Albert's Reunion' and 'St George and the Dragon', which are shown with the year of their first public performance. More detailed information about individual recordings is given in the Discography from page 89 onwards.

In compiling this material, a third of which has never previously been published, I am indebted to a number of individuals. My special thanks are due to Chris Morgan and Derek Bromberg at the BBC for their help in tracing rare recorded material. I am also grateful to my secretaries, Anne Buckingham and Priscilla Keith, for grappling with the problems of transcription and northern dialect. I appreciate, too, my editor Roger Houghton's flexible and devoted work on the project and I have been greatly helped, as always, by the encouragement and support of my wife, Caroline.

Finally, my special thanks to both Stanley and Laney Holloway for their hospitality and enthusiastic co-operation without which – as my dedication indicates – this book would not exist.

The author and publishers would also like to thank the following for their kind permission to reproduce copyright material in this book: Francis Day & Hunter Ltd for *Old Sam* © 1929; *Beat The Retreat On Thy Drum* © 1931; *Marksman Sam* © 1934; *Sam's Medal* © 1933; *The Lion and Albert* © 1932; *The Return of Albert* © 1934; *Runcorn Ferry* © 1933; *The Jubilee Sov'rin* © 1937; *Albert And The 'Eadsman* © 1937; *The Recumbent Posture* © 1939; *The Battle Of Hastings* © 1937; *Gunner Joe* © 1933; *The Magna Charter* © 1937; *With Her Head Tucked Underneath Her Arm* © 1934; *The 'Ole In The Ark* © 1937; *Brahn Boots* © 1940; *Three Ha'pence A Foot* © 1932; *St George And The Dragon* © 1935; *Jonah And The Grampus* © 1937; *Uppards* © 1941; *Sweeney Todd, The Barber* © 1935; Stanley Holloway/EMI Music Publishing Ltd for *'Alt! Who Goes There?* ©

PART ONE

Sam Small

OLD SAM
(Sam, Pick Oop Tha' Musket)
by Stanley Holloway (1929)

It occurred on the evening before Waterloo
And troops were lined up on Parade,
And Sergeant inspecting 'em, he was a terror
Of whom every man was afraid –

All excepting one man who was in the front rank,
A man by the name of Sam Small,
And 'im and the Sergeant were both 'daggers drawn',
They thought 'nowt' of each other at all.

As Sergeant walked past he was swinging his arm,
And he happened to brush against Sam,
And knocking his musket clean out of his hand
It fell to the ground with a slam.

'Pick it oop,' said Sergeant, abrupt like but cool,
But Sam with a shake of his head
Said, 'Seeing as tha' knocked it out of me hand,
P'raps tha'll pick the thing oop instead.'

'Sam, Sam, pick oop tha' musket,'
The Sergeant exclaimed with a roar.
Sam said 'Tha' knocked it doon, Reet!
Then tha'll pick it oop, or it stays where it is, on't floor.'

The sound of high words
Very soon reached the ears of an Officer, Lieutenant Bird,
Who says to the Sergeant, 'Now what's all this 'ere?'
And the Sergeant told what had occurred.

'Sam, Sam, pick oop tha' musket,'
Lieutenant exclaimed with some heat.
Sam said 'He knocked it doon, Reet! then he'll pick it oop,
Or it stays where it is, at me feet.'

It caused quite a stir when the Captain arrived
To find out the cause of the trouble;
And every man there, all excepting Old Sam,
Was full of excitement and bubble.

'Sam, Sam, pick oop tha' musket,'
Said Captain for strictness renowned.
Sam said 'He knocked it doon, Reet!
Then he'll pick it oop, or it stays where it is on't ground.'

The same thing occurred when the Major and Colonel
Both tried to get Sam to see sense,
But when Old Duke o' Wellington came into view
Well, the excitement was tense.

Up rode the Duke on a lovely white 'orse,
To find out the cause of the bother;
He looks at the musket and then at old Sam
And he talked to Old Sam like a brother,

'Sam, Sam, pick oop tha' musket,'
The Duke said as quiet as could be,
'Sam, Sam, pick oop tha' musket
Coom on, lad, just to please me.'

'Alright, Duke,' said Old Sam, 'just for thee I'll oblige,
And to show thee I meant no offence.'
So Sam picked it up, 'Gradeley, lad,' said the Duke,
'Right-o, boys, let battle commence.'

First performed at the London Palladium in 1929. Recorded in 1930.

'ALT! WHO GOES THERE?
by Stanley Holloway (1930)

Old Sam first came to London
When George the Fourth were King,
He'd been in th'Army, man and boy
For twenty year come Spring.

The troops were lined up on parade
And Sergeant, says 'Eh, Sam,
T'neet tha' goes on sentry-go
At t'Palace, Buckingham.'

So off goes Sam to Palace gates
His chest puffed out with pride,
With musket on his shoulder
He walks up and down, outside.

A crowd soon thronged around him
And caused a fearful jam –
Some come to look at King and Queen
Some come to look at Sam.

Sam stood there cold and haughty-like
With dignity sublime.
Some asks 'Were you at Waterloo?'
And some asks 'What's the time?'

When suddenly from out of crowd
A chap walks bold and straight,
He crosses right in front of Sam
And tries to open gate.

Old Sam says ''Alt! And who goes there?
Who'se thee does tha' suppose?'
The stranger answers 'George the Fourth.
I live in 'ere, tha' knows.'

Old Sam says 'Does think I'm daft?
Don't try to tell me that.
If thou art King – then where's thee Crown?
Tha'rt wearing bowler hat.'

'That's right,' says King. 'That's right enough,
It's strange to thee no doubt,
But Ah put on bowler hat
'Cos it t'were raining when I comes out.'

'Oh well,' said Sam. 'Ah suppose you're right,
I didn't know t'were thee.'
The King says 'No offence, me lad,
Come in for a cup o' tea.'

'I'd like a cup of tea,' said Sam,
'Ah don't mind if I do.'
The Queen pours cup of tea and says,
'How many lumps, Sam? Two?'

They chatted there for 'alf an hour
When knock come at the door,
The King he goes
And finds the Duke of Wellington there, for sure.

'Good Afternoon,' says Duke of Wellington,
'Is Sam with thee?'
'Aye, he is an' all,' says King,
'He's having a cup o' tea.'

'Well that's a pretty thing,' says Duke,
'That's pretty, I declare.'
He catches sight of Sam and says,
'Sam, what's thar doing in there?'

Sam comes to door all jumpy like
And red as anything.

'Ah'm doing nothing, Duke,' he cries,
'But having tea with King.'

'Ah thought as there was summut up,'
The Duke coldly replied,
'Because I see thee musket
Leaning against rails outside.'

'Some clumsy chap had knocked it down
It give me quite a scare,
So I stooped down and picked it up
Seeing as thee weren't there.'

'You stooped and picked me musket up?' said Sam,
'Well, I declare,
And thee with thy lumbago, too,
I'll bet it made thee swear.'

'I'll not wait for second cup,' said Sam,
'Ah'll come with thee.
So Goodnight both your Majesties, and long live both your
    Majesties
And when tha's next in Lancashire, tha's tea's with me.'

BEAT THE RETREAT ON THY DRUM!
(Sam, Sam, Beat the Retreat)
by R. P. Weston and Bert Lee (1931)

I'm hundred and two today, bagoom!
Eh, today, I'm a hundred and two,
And at ten years of age, I wor soldiering, aye,
I wor drummer boy at Waterloo.

And when Wellington said 'Sam, my lad, get thy drum,'
I wor so mighty anxious to start
That I dashed on in front and got captured by French,
And wor taken afore Boneyparte.

And Boneyparte, scratching his-self under t'arm,
Like you see him in pictures today
Said '*Voila*! so you are a drummer boy, *oui*?
Then show me how well you can play.'

'Sam, Sam! beat the Retreat! Beat the Retreat on thy drum,
I said 'Beat the what?' He said, 'Beat the Retreat.'
I said 'Nay, that's one thing as I'll never beat;
I'll beat ye the Charge, or I'll beat the Tattoo,
But I'm British and Yorkshire, ba goom!
And though you're Napoleon, I'll see thee blowed
If I'll beat the Retreat on my drum!

Then scratching his-self under t'arm once again,
In the way Boneyparte always did,
He said, 'Sacré bloo!' which is French for 'Ba goom',
'Eh, thou hast got a sauce for a kid.'

Then he called Josephine (Josephine wor his Queen)
And he said 'Tell this lad, Josephine,
If he don't beat Retreat on his drum,
He'll be shot – aye and put underneath Guil-li-o-tine.'

So she put her arm round me, and stroking me 'air,
She whispered, 'Hush, hush now – coom, coom!
Be a good lad – do as Boneyparte tells thee,
And beat the Retreat on thy drum!'

I said 'Missus, nay!' then she started to cry,
And she murmured 'O, lad, you are too sweet to die;
And hast thou a mother who loves thee?' she sobbed.
I said 'Aye, and she's Yorkshire, ba goom!
And she'd beat the Retreat on me trousers
If I were to beat the Retreat on me drum!'

Then Boneyparte scratching his-self once again
Said 'My lad, I've a Mother like her,'
And taking his medals off with his two hands
And unpinning his gold Croix de Guerre
He put them on me, kissed me on both cheeks,
Then pulled me outside of the tent,
And leading me up to his Army,

And scratching his-self undert'arm as he went,
'Soldiers of France,' he cried,
'This is Sam Small, he's a hero though only a kid,
E-coutez, mes braves, et com-prenez toute suite!
What do you think this lad did?'

'Beat the Retreat on thy drum! said I,
Beat the Retreat on thy drum!
And this lad refused, though I said he should die;
Why did he refuse?' I said 'I'll them 'em why:
For two reasons I wouldn't beat the Retreat
Though I knew that it meant kingdom come;
One reason was somebody pinched both me sticks,
And the other, I'd busted me drum!'

ONE EACH APIECE ALL ROUND
by Stanley Holloway (1931)

No. 2468
Private Samuel Small
Were up before his Captain
To explain away a brawl.

The Captain said 'Now state your case,
But please be short and brief,
Tell everything that happened
To the best of your belief.'

'Well now,' said Sam, 'it's like this 'ere
Me and some other chaps
Had a little celebration
And a drink or two perhaps.

'It happened to be me birthday,
And on counting out I found
I'd got enough out of me pay
To have one apiece all round.

'We drank 'em up, no heeltaps
And then the same again,
"Here's a health unto his Majesty,"
We sang, "long may he reign."

'With chorus after chorus
We made the walls resound,
And then to keep things going
We had one each apiece all round.

'It were nearly time for lights out
And getting rather late,
We had no money left for drinks
So we put 'em on the slate.

'Suddenly out went the lights
Without the slightest warning,
We all trooped out but not without
A bottle for the morning.

'Across the barrack square we went
As bold as any gentry,
It was a lark when in the dark
We come across a sentry.

'"'Alt, who goes there?" the sentry cried,
We firmly stood our ground.
"It's only Sam," I cried, "and we've had
One each apiece all round,

'"We've been drinking . . . drinking . . . drinking."
We got into the barrack room and started to undress,
Just then the Sergeant came along,
Straight from the Sergeants' Mess.

'We shut the door, sat on the floor,
We never made a sound
And to finish off me birthday,
We had one each apiece all round.'

'Well, Private Small,' said Captain,
'I shall have to punish thee

For this grave misdemeanour,
You will get ten days' CB.'

'Ten days CB,' said Samuel,
'That's heavy I'll be bound.'
Said Captain 'Split among your pals,
It's one each apiece all round.'

SAM'S MEDAL

by Mabel Constanduros and Michael Hogan (1933)

You've 'eard of Samuel Small, per'aps?
    A lad of bull-dog breed,
'Oo saved 'is Sergeant-Major's life;
    (A most *unusual* deed).
At Waterloo 'e fought and bled,
    And when the war was won,
The King a medal struck for Sam,
    Because of what 'e'd done.

So Sam came up to Palace Gates,
    In famous London Town;
A Sentry in a Busby 'at
    Was walkin' up and down.

The Sentry stopped and looked at Sam,
    'Excuse me, mate,' said he.
'Might you be Private Samuel Small?'
    And Sam said, 'Ay, that's me!'
'Well, go on in,' said Sentry, 'Quick!'
    And gave the gate a slam,
'King's got a medal there for thee!'
    'I know 'e 'as,' said Sam.

Well, Sam pushed open Palace Door
    And stood in 'oly 'ush;
He found himself inside a room,
    All marble busts and plush.

Archbishop in a red cocked 'at,
    And breeches white and blue,
Said, 'Is your name Sam Small, my lad?'
    'It is,' said Sam. ''Ow do!'

'Don't loiter, then,' says Bishop, sharp,
    'Like nursemaid wi' a pram.
The King's got medal there for thee.'
    'I know 'e 'as!' said Sam.

Upstairs Sam met Prime Minister,
    A top-'at on 'is 'ead.
'Is trousers they was velveteen;
    One leg was blue – one red.

'E glanced at Sam all 'aughty-like
    And asked 'im, 'Might you be
A man called Private Samuel Small?'
    And Sam said, 'Ay, that's me.'

'Well, don't keep King all night,' 'e said,
    'Surprised at thee, I am.
'E's got thy medal there, 'as King.'
    'I KNOW 'e 'as,' said Sam.

But when Sam came on King and Queen,
    His awe he couldn't smother;
For there sat King – one hand held th' orb
    And sceptre was in t'other.

Sam grasped the situation like
    In less than half a jiff,
He gave a very smart salute
    And knocked his 'at skew-whiff.

'Tha' must be Samuel Small,' said King.
    'That's reet,' said Sam, 'I am.'
'Well, I've a medal 'ere for thee.'
    'I KNOW thou 'ast,' said Sam.

11

'Don't be impatient, Sam,' says King,
  'Before 'tis 'anded you,
There's certain grave formalities
  Which must be gotten through.

'The V.C.'s granted Samuel Small
  (The King began to read),
For savin' Sergeant-Major's life;
  (A most *unusual* deed).

'Dragged 'im to safety under fire
  When serving in the line.
Now tell me, Sam, 'ow came you do
  This deed so brave and fine?'

'Well now,' said Sam, ''twas like this 'ere –
  That Sergeant-Major come
Towards our trenches, very drunk,
  A-wavin' jar of rum.

'And just as we was lettin' forth
  A loud triumphant shout,
A darned great gun – excuse me, Queen –
  Went off and laid 'im out.

'I rushed and grabbed the precious jar;
  'E seized me round the 'tum
(Your pardon, Queen). So 'e got saved
  As well as jar of rum!'

'But if there'd been no rum,' said King,
  'Though death might sound his knell,
Thou would'st 'ave done that same brave deed?'
  'I would!' said Sam. 'Like 'ell!'

'Did you 'ear that?' said King to Queen.
  She said, 'Indeed I did!'
'Don't give 'im ruddy medal then!'
  And nor they never did.

OLD SAM'S PARTY

by Mabel Constanduros (1933)

Sam Small, though approaching his eightieth year
Were feeling all brisk-like and hearty,
So he sent out an invite when Christmas drew near
And asked all his friends to a party.

There was old ale and sandwiches, beef and cold tongue,
And trifle with gooseberry jam,
And parkin and humbugs, a couple of ducks,
And lovely great platefuls of ham.

Sam's Captain were there from his old army days,
A man for his strictness renowned,
And Left. Bird and the Sergeant, the same
Who once knocked Sam's musket on t'ground.

First Left. Bird volunteered for a song,
And accompanied by Sergeant McNally,
Sang 'Of all the girls that are so smart
There's none like pretty Sally.'

Then Captain jumped up, said he'd not be outdone,
He played for himself with one finger.
There were tears in all eyes when he'd finished his song;
He were a magnificent singer.

He'd start a bit husky, but nothing to last,
His voice cleared up fine when he'd coughed:
'Faithful below, Tom did his duty,
And now he's gone aloft, and now he's gone aloft.'

As his last trembling note died away in a gulp
Came a clatter of hoofs from outside.
Sam pulled back the blind and flushed up to his ears,
'It's the Duke!' he announced with much pride.

And it were. Up he rode on his lovely white horse.
Sam faltered 'Why, Duke, is it you?

And thee with lumbago and snow on the ground.
I take it most kind, that I do.'

'Gradely, lad,' said the Duke, condescending and kind.
'By Gum, but how well you do look.
Er, this room's a bit stuffy and hot. Do you mind
If I hang up me coat on this hook?'

Then a thunderous banging was heard on t'door
And bell gave a furious ring.
They all turned quite pale as a voice from outside
Cried 'Open in t'name of the King.'

Sam opened the door. There he stood, George IV,
A model of beauty and grace.
His crown on his head and sceptre in hand,
And behind him stood Queen with a mace.

'Thee told us,' said King, 'when we come up thy way
To call and take pot luck with thee.
And seeing as we're up for the cup-tie tha' knows
The Queen and me's popped in to tea.'

They hung up their crowns on the stand in the hall.
Sam paid off their cab, eighteen pence.
The Queen parked her mace in Sam's umbrella stand, ,
'Now,' she said, 'let party commence.'

Then they all clapped their hands and sung out aloud,
Demanding a speech from their host.
And Sam, very bashful, said 'Well I don't mind.
Fill t'glasses, I'll give thee a toast.

'Now friends, here's a health to all those that I love,
And a health to all those that love me.
A health to all those that love those that I love
And to those that love those that love me.'

MARKSMAN SAM

by Marriott Edgar (1934)

When Sam Small joined the regiment,
   'E were no' but a raw recruit;
And they marched 'im away one wint'ry day
   'Is musket course to shoot.

They woke 'im up at the crack o' dawn,
   Wi' many a nudge and shake;
'E were dreaming that t' Sergeant 'ad broke 'is neck,
   And 'e didn't want to wake.

Lieutenant Bird came on parade,
   And chided the lads for mooning.
'E talked in a voice like a pound o' plums,
   'Is tonsils needed pruning.

'Move to the right by fours,' 'e said,
   Crisp-like but *most severe*,
But Sam didn't know 'is right from 'is left,
   So pretended 'e didn't 'ear.

Said Lieutenant, 'Sergeant – take that man's name,'
   The Sergeant took out 'is pencil,
'E were getting ashamed o' taking Sam's name,
   And were thinking o' cutting a stencil.

Sam carried a musket, a knapsack and coat,
   Spur boots that 'e'd managed to wangle,
A 'atchet, a spade – in fact, as Sam said,
   'E'd got everything bar t'kitchen mangle.

'March easy, men,' Lieutenant cried,
   As the musket range grew near,
'March easy me blushing Aunt Fanny,' said Sam,
   'What a chance with all this 'ere.'

When they told 'im to fire at five 'undred yards,
   Sam nearly 'ad a fit,

For a six-foot wall, or the Albert 'All,
    Were all 'e were likely to 'it.

'E 'ad fitted a cork in 'is musket end
    To keep 'is powder dry;
And 'e didn't remember to tak' it out
    The first time 'e let fly.

'Is gun went off wi' a kind of pop!
    Where 'is bullet went no one knew,
But next day they spoke of a tinker's moke
    Being killed by a cork near Crewe.

At three 'undred yards, Sam shut 'is eyes
    And took a careful aim;
'E failed to score, but the marker swore
    And walked away quite lame.

At two 'undred yards, Sam fired so wild,
    That the Sergeant feared for 'is skin,
And the lads all cleared int' t'neighbouring field
    And started to dig 'emselves in.

'Ooh, Sergeant! I hear a scraping noise,'
    Said Sam, 'What can it be?'
The noise that 'e 'eard were Lieutenant Bird,
    'Oo were climbing the nearest tree.

'Ooh, Sergeant!' said Sam, 'I've 'it the bull!
    What price my shooting now?'
Said the Sergeant, 'A bull? Yer gormless fool,
    Yon isn't a bull, it's a cow!'

At fifty yards 'is musket kicked,
    And went off with a noise like a blizzard,
And down came a crow looking fair surprised
    With 'is ram-rod through its gizzard.

As 'e loaded 'is musket to fire agen,
    Said the Sergeant, 'Don't waste shot!
Yer'd best fix bayonets and charge, my lad,
    It's the only chance yer've got!'

Sam kept loading 'is gun while the Sergeant spoke
  Till the bullets peeped out at the muzzle,
When all of a sudden it went off bang!
  What made it go off were a puzzle.

The bullets flew out in a kind of spray,
  And everything round got peppered.
When they counted 'is score,
  'E'd got eight bulls-eyes, four magpies, two lambs and a
    shepherd.

And the Sergeant for this got a D.C.M.
  And the Colonel an O.B.E.
Lieutenant Bird got the D.S.O.
  And Sam got – five days' C.B.

SAM DRUMMED OUT
by R. P. Weston and Bert Lee (1935)

Whan a lad's been drummed out of the Army,
He's an outcast despised by all men;
I'd rather be shot at dawn any old time
'Cause I never get up before ten.

Once I was drummed out, tho' today I'm a hero
With all that a soldier could wish.
Ay, once poor old Sam stood before a Court Martial
With head bowed in shame and anguish.

And the old Colonel said, when he 'eard the charge read,
'It's a terrible crime, Sam,' said he,
And the whisper went round 'Has old Sam
Been a traitor to his King and his country?'

Nay, nay, I was charged with a crime worse than that,
Far more dastardly wicked and mean.
I were charged with maliciously putting cold water
In beer in the Sergeant's canteen.

17

And the Colonel's voice shook and he swallowed a lump
And he said 'Nay, nay, come, come, ee dear, dear,
Good beer is the lifeblood of our glorious army
Our battles was all won on beer.'

'What have you got to say to this terrible charge?'
I said 'Nowt.'
He said 'Nowt?'
I said 'Nowt.'

He said 'Can't you say owt but nowt?'
I said 'No, nowt.'
'Well,' he said, 'Sam,
Then you'll be drummed out.'

Next morning the company lined on parade
I stood at attention quite stiff;
Then the Sergeant stepped forward and knocked off my pillbox
And worse – he untidied me quiff.

Then he pulled out his sword and cut off me coat buttons
Them buttons fell 'clink' on the floor;
But when he began on me trousers I said,
'Don't lower me prestige any more.'

Then he pulled off me medals, me twenty-five medals
I'd won out in different parts.
But I said to him 'Oi, give me two of them back,
'Cause I won them there two playing darts.'

Then the drums and the pipes played the Rogues March
And the Colonel he sobbed and said 'Sam,
You're no longer a Soldier, I'm sorry to say
Sam, Sam, you're a dirty old man.'

And soon I was outside the old barrack gates
With the tears rolling all down me face;
Then up rode the Colonel's young daughter, God bless her,
The pride of the Regiment, our Grace.

She said 'What's to do, Sam?'
I said 'What's to do, I'm drummed out lass for watering beer.'

Then she fell off her 'orse, threw her arms round me neck
And said 'Sam, you poor innocent dear.'

Then she rushed to her father, the Colonel, and said,
'Say, papa, I'll hand you the dope.
Poor Sam here is innocent, I did the deed
I was told to by my Band of Hope.'

Then the Colonel said 'Corporal Sam, please come back.'
I said 'Nay, nay, I've just been drummed out.'
Then the Colonel said 'Sergeant Sam, Sergeant Sam, please.'
I just shrugged and said 'Nowt doing, nowt.'

He said 'Lieutenant Sam, come forgive and forget.'
But I stamped and said 'Nay, nay begone.'
Then he said 'Captain Sam.'
I said 'Captain, tut tut, make it Major and then I'll clock on.'

And that's how I won me Commission, me lads,
A commission I think I well earned –
10 per cent on the beer, 10 per cent on the stout
And the pennies on bottles returned.

And the Regiment gave me a tankard inscribed with
    these words
Which I'm proud of, I am
'Presented by First Lancashire Fuisilliers
To their champion liar, old Sam.'

SAM'S STURGEON

by Ashley Sterne (1935)

Sam Small were fishing in canal
'Twixt Manchester and Sale;
He hadn't had a bite all day
And nought to sup but ale.

Then all at once his fishing line
Went rushing out like mad;
'By gum,' cried Sam, 'I've got a bite,'
So by gum he 'ad.

He tugged and tugged and better tugged
His line it rose and sank;
Then fish gave one last dying gasp
And flopped stone dead on t'bank.

Then a policeman bustled up
On feet both large and flat.
He looked at Sam, he looked at fish
And said 'Ee, who done that?'

'It's just a sort of fish,' said Sam
'I'm taking home to tea.'
'Tha's not,' said policeman. 'That tha's not,
It don't belong to thee.
'It's what they call a Sturgeon, Sam,
That fish belongs to King,
So take it up the Palace, lad,
As fast as anything.'

Sam stooped and picked the Sturgeon up
Well knowing who was boss;
Then ran to station where he bought
Two tickets for King's Cross.

When Sam reached London Town
The crowd all raised a cheering cry;
The traffic parted left and right
To let that Sturgeon by.

The Palace sentry, haughty like, said
'What might be your wish?'
But when he saw what Sam had brought
He cried 'Pass, Royal fish.'

Sam knocked at door and servant girl said,
'Step inside the hall,
The King and Queen is out,' says she,
'But not for thee, Sam Small.'

And so with Sturgeon in his arms
Sam tramped up corridor,

He trailed along some passages
And knocked at parlour door.

'Come in,' says King,
So Sam went in with Royal fish and all.
'Why dash me buttons,' cries the King
'If it isn't old Sam Small.'

'That's me,' said Sam, 'and 'ere's a fish
Our policeman said were thine;
A Sturgeon caught in Ship Canal
With rod and hook and line.'

'Well, well,' said King, 'come sit thee down,
Tha' must be fair done up.
We just were going to have us teas,
Tha'll stay and have a sup?'

'Thanks, King,' said Sam and takes a seat
With fish upon his knee.
'Nay, put that thing on sofa, Sam,' says King,
'And have thy tea.'

'Now what about this fish?' asks Sam,
But King he whispers low,
'I'm going to tell thee something, Sam,
But don't let policeman know.

'I hate to show ingratitude
And please don't think me mean,
But I never did like Sturgeon, Sam,
Nor, come to that, does Queen.

'To eat the stuff we hate so much
Well, Sam, we find it hard;
So we hand 'em to the Chamberlain
Who stacks them in back yard.

'Just thee look out that window, Sam,
And see where t'Sturgeons go.'
Sam looked at yard and saw 'em all
In thousands in a row.

'It's champion seeing thee again,
But Sam twixt me and thee
I can't stand Sturgeons
But I love a kipper to me tea.'

'Now fancy that,' says Sam, 'by gum,
Why them's my favourite fish.'
And then the Queen came smiling in,
With kippers on the dish.

'Do you know Sam Small, my dear?' says King.
Queen says 'Why, yes, yes, yes,
Just touch the bell and tell our James
To bring more watercress.'

'Think on,' says King when tea were done
And Sam got up to go,
'Kippers is what I like for tea
But don't let policeman know.'

So Sam went home to Lancashire
And said a silent prayer,
With blessings on the kippered fish
'Long live the Royal Pair.'

OLD SAM'S CHRISTMAS PUDDING

by Marriott Edgar (1939)

It was Christmas Day in the trenches
In Spain in Penninsula War,
And Sam Small were cleaning his musket
A thing as he ne'er done before.

They'd had 'em inspected that morning,
And Sam had got into disgrace
For when Sergeant had looked down the barrel
A sparrow flew out in his face.

The Sergeant reported the matter
To Lieutenant Bird then and there.

Said Lieutenant 'How very disgusting
The Duke must be told of this 'ere.'

The Duke were upset when he heard,
He said 'I'm astonished, I am.
I must make a most drastic example
There'll be no Christmas pudding for Sam.'

When Sam were informed of his sentence
Surprise rooted him to the spot –
'Twere much worse than he had expected,
He thought as he'd only be shot.

And so he sat cleaning his musket,
And polishing barrel and butt,
Whilst the pudding his mother had sent him
Lay there in the mud at his foot.

Now the centre that Sam's lot were holding
Ran around a place called Badajoz
Where the Spaniards had put up a bastion
And ooh what a bastion it was!

They pounded away all the morning
With canister, grape shot and ball,
But the face of the bastion defied them
They made no impression at all.

They started again after dinner
Bombarding as hard as they could;
And the Duke brought his own private cannon
But that weren't a ha'pence o' good.

The Duke said 'Sam, put down thy musket
And help me to lay this gun true.'
Sam answered 'You'd best ask your favours
From them as you give pudding to.'

The Duke looked at Sam so reproachful
'And don't take it that way,' said he,
'Us Generals have got to be ruthless
It hurts me more than it did thee.'

Sam sniffed at these words kind of sceptic,
Then looked down the Duke's private gun
And said 'We'd best put in two charges
We'll never bust bastion with one.'

He tipped cannon ball out of muzzle,
He took out the wadding and all,
He filled barrel chock full of powder,
Then picked up and replaced the ball.
He took a good aim at the bastion
Then said 'Right-o, Duke, let her fly.'
The cannon nigh jumped off her trunnions
And up went the bastion, sky high.

The Duke he weren't 'alf elated,
He danced round the trench full of glee
And said 'Sam, for this gallant action
You can hot up your pudding for tea.'

Sam looked round to pick up his pudding,
But it wasn't there, nowhere about.
In the place where he thought he had left it
Lay the cannon ball he'd just tipped out.

Sam saw in a flash what 'ad happened:
By an unprecedented mishap
The pudding his mother had sent him
Had blown Badajoz off the map.

That's why Fuisilliers wear to this moment
A badge which they think's a grenade,
But they're wrong – it's a brass reproduction
Of the pudding Sam's mother once made.

SAM GOES TO IT

by Marriott Edgar (1941)

Sam Small had retired from the Army
In the old Duke of Wellington's time,
So when present unpleasantness started
He were what you might call past his prime.

He'd lived for some years in retirement
And knew nowt of the war, if you please,
Till they blasted and bombed his allotment
And shelled the best part of his peas.

T'were as if bugles called Sam to duty
For his musket he started to search;
He found it at last in the hen house
Buff Orpingtons had it for perch.

Straight off to the Fusilliers' depot
He went to rejoin his old troop –
Where he found as they couldn't recruit him
Until his age group was called up.

Now Sam wasn't getting no younger,
Past the three score and ten mark was he,
And he reckoned by time they reached his group
He'd be very near ten score and three.

So he took up the matter with Churchill
Who said 'I don't know what to do,
Never was there a time when so many
Came asking so much of so few.'

'I don't want no favours,' Sam answered,
'Don't think as I'm one of that mob.
All I'm asking is give me the tools, lad,
And let me help finish the job.'

'I'll fit you in somewhere,' said Winnie,
'Old Soldiers we must not discard.'
Then seeing he'd got his own musket
He sent him to join the Home Guard.

They gave Sam a coat with no stripes on,
In spite of the service he'd seen
Which considering he'd been a King's Sergeant
Kind of rankled – you see what I mean.

He said 'I come back to the Army
Expecting my country's thanks,

And the first thing I find when I get here
Is that I've been reduced to the ranks.'

He found all the lads sympathetic,
They agreed that it t'were a disgrace
Except one old chap in the corner
With a nutcracker kind of a face.

Said the old feller 'Who do you think you are?
The last to appear on the scene,
And you start off by wanting promotion
Last come, last served – see what I mean?'

Said Sam 'Wasn't I at Corunna,
And when company commander got shot
Didn't I lead battalion to victory?'
Said the old fella 'No you did not.'

'I didn't?' said Sam quite indignent
'Why, in every fight Wellington fought
Wasn't I at his right hand to guard him?'
Said old chap 'You were nowt of the sort.'

'What do you know of Duke and his battles?'
Said Sam with a withering look.
Said the old man 'I ought to know something,
Between you and me, I'm the Duke.'

And if you should look in any evening,
You'll find them both in the canteen,
Ex Commander-in-Chief and ex Sergeant
Both just Home Guards – you see what I mean?

PART TWO

Albert Ramsbottom

THE LION AND ALBERT
by Marriott Edgar (1932)

There's a famous seaside place called Blackpool,
    That's noted for fresh air and fun,
And Mr and Mrs Ramsbottom
    Went there with young Albert, their son.

A grand little lad was young Albert,
    All dressed in his best; quite a swell
With a stick with an 'orse's 'ead 'andle,
    The finest that Woolworth's could sell.

They didn't think much to the Ocean:
    The waves, they was fiddlin' and small,
There was no wrecks and nobody drownded,
    Fact, nothing to laugh at at all.

So, seeking for further amusement,
    They paid and went into the Zoo,
Where they'd Lions and Tigers and Camels,
    And old ale and sandwiches too.

There were one great big Lion called Wallace;
    His nose were all covered with scars –
He lay in a somnolent posture,
    With the side of his face on the bars.

Now Albert had heard about Lions,
 How they was ferocious and wild –
To see Wallace lying so peaceful,
 Well, it didn't seem right to the child.

So straightway the brave little feller,
 Not showing a morsel of fear,
Took his stick with its 'orse's 'ead 'andle
 And pushed it in Wallace's ear.

You could see that the Lion didn't like it,
 For giving a kind of a roll,
He pulled Albert inside the cage with 'im,
 And swallowed the little lad 'ole.

Then Pa, who had seen the occurrence,
 And didn't know what to do next,
Said 'Mother! Yon Lion's 'et Albert',
 And Mother said 'Well, I am vexed!'

Then Mr and Mrs Ramsbottom –
 Quite rightly, when all's said and done –
Complained to the Animal Keeper,
 That the Lion had eaten their son.

The keeper was quite nice about it;
 He said 'What a nasty mishap.
Are you sure that it's *your* boy he's eaten?'
 Pa said 'Am I sure? There's his cap!'

The manager had to be sent for.
 He came and he said 'What's to do?'
Pa said 'Yon Lion's 'et Albert,'
 And 'im in his Sunday clothes, too.'

Then Mother said, 'Right's right, young feller;
 I think it's a shame and a sin,
For a lion to go and eat Albert,
 And after we've paid to come in.'

The manager wanted no trouble,
 He took out his purse right away,

ALWAYS DOING IT WAS HE?

Saying 'How much to settle the matter?'
    And Pa said 'What do you usually pay?'

But Mother had turned a bit awkward
    When she thought where her Albert had gone.
She said 'No! someone's got to be summonsed' –
    So that was decided upon.

Then off they went to the P'lice Station,
    In front of the Magistrate chap;
They told 'im what happened to Albert,
    And proved it by showing his cap.

The Magistrate gave his opinion
    That no one was really to blame
And he said that he hoped the Ramsbottoms
    Would have further sons to their name.

At that Mother got proper blazing,
    'And thank you, sir, kindly,' said she.
'What waste all our lives raising children
    To feed ruddy Lions? Not me!'

THE RETURN OF ALBERT
(Albert Comes Back)
by Marriott Edgar (1934)

You've 'eard 'ow young Albert Ramsbottom,
    In the Zoo up at Blackpool one year,
With a stick and 'orse's 'ead 'andle,
    Gave a lion a poke in the ear.

The name of the lion was Wallace,
    The poke in the ear made 'im wild;
And before you could say 'Bob's your Uncle,'
    'E'd up and 'e'd swallered the child.

'E were sorry the moment 'e'd done it,
    With children 'e'd always been chums,
And besides, 'e'd no teeth in 'is noddle,
    And 'e couldn't chew Albert on t'gums.

'E could feel the lad moving inside 'im,
    As 'e lay on 'is bed of dried ferns,
And it might 'ave been little lad's birthday,
    'E wished 'im such 'appy returns.

But Albert kept kicking and fighting,
    Till Wallace arose feeling bad,
And felt it were time that 'e started to stage
    A come-back for the lad.

So with 'is 'ead down in a corner,
    On 'is front paws 'e started to walk,
And 'e coughed and 'e sneezed and 'e gargled,
    Till Albert shot out like a cork.

Old Wallace felt better direc'ly,
    And 'is figure once more became lean,
But the only difference with Albert
    Was 'is face and 'is 'ands were quite clean.

Meanwhile Mister and Missus Ramsbottom
    'Ad gone 'ome to tea feeling blue;
Ma says 'I feel down in the mouth like,'
    Pa says 'Aye! I bet Albert does too.'

Said Ma 'It just goes for to show yer
    That the future is never revealed,
If I thought we was going to lose 'im
    I'd 'ave not 'ad 'is boots soled and 'eeled.

'Let's look on the bright side,' said Father
    'What can't be 'elped must be endured,
Every cloud 'as a silvery lining,
    And we did 'ave young Albert insured.'

A knock at the door came that moment,
    As Father these kind words did speak,

'Twas the man from t'Prudential,
    E'd called for their 'tuppence per person per week.'

When Father saw who 'ad been knocking,
    'E laughed and 'e kept laughing so,
That the young man said 'What's there to laugh at?'
    Pa said 'You'll laugh an' all when you know.'

'Excuse 'im for laughing,' said Mother,
    'But really things 'appen so strange,
Our Albert's been ate by a lion,
    You've got to pay us for a change.'

Said the young feller from the Prudential,
    'Now, come come, let's understand this,
You don't mean to say that you've lost 'im?'
    Ma says 'Oh, no! we *know* where 'e is.'

When the young man 'ad 'eard all the details,
    A bag from 'is pocket he drew,
And 'e paid them with int'rest and bonus,
    The sum of nine pounds four and two.

Pa 'ad scarce got 'is 'and on the money,
    When a face at the window they see,
And Mother says 'Eeh! look, it's Albert,'
    And Father says 'Aye, it *would* be.'

Young Albert came in all excited,
    And started 'is story to give,
And Pa says 'I'll never trust lions again,
    Not as long as I live.'

The young feller from the Prudential
    To pick up the money began,
And Father says 'Eeh! just a moment,
    Don't be in a hurry, young man.'

Then giving young Albert a shilling,
    He said 'Pop off back to the Zoo.
'Ere's yer stick with the 'orse's 'ead 'andle,
    Go and see what the Tigers can do!'

RUNCORN FERRY
(Tuppence Per Person Per Trip)
by Marriott Edgar (1933)

On the banks of the Mersey, over on Cheshire side,
    Lies Runcorn that's best known to fame
By Transporter Bridge as tak's folks over its stream,
    Or else brings 'em back across same.

In days afore Transporter Bridge were put up
    A Ferry Boat lay in the slip,
And old Ted the Boatman would row folks across
    At per tuppence per person per trip.

Now Runcorn lay over on one side of stream
    And Widnes on t'other side stood,
And as nobody wanted to go either place –
    Well, the trade wasn't any too good.

One ev'ning to Ted's superlative surprise
    Three customers came into view –
A Mister and Missus Ramsbottom it were,
    And Albert, their little son, too.

''Ow much for the three?' Mister Ramsbottom asked,
    As 'is 'and to 'is pocket did dip.
Ted said 'Same for three as it would be for one:
    Per tuppence per person per trip.'

'Y' not charging tuppence for that little lad?'
    Said Mother, her eyes flashing wild.
'Per tuppence per person per trip,' answered Ted,
    'Per woman, per man, or per child.'

'Fivepence for three, that's the most that I'll pay,'
    Said Father, 'Don't waste time in t'talk.'
'Per tuppence per person per trip,' answered Ted,
    'And them as can't pay 'as to walk.'

'We can walk an' all,' said Father.
    'Come, Mother, it's none so deep, t'weather's quite
      mild.'

So into the water the three of them stepped –
    The father, the mother, the child.

The further they paddled the deeper it got,
    But they wouldn't give in once t'begun;
In the spirit that's made Lancashire what it is
    They'd sooner be drownded than done.

Very soon the old people were up to their necks
    And the little lad clean out of sight.
Said Father, 'Where's Albert?' and Mother replied,
    'I've got 'old of 'is 'and, 'e's all right.'

'T were just at that moment Pa got an idea,
    And floundering back to old Ted,
'E said, 'We've walked that way –
    Come, tak' us the rest for half-price, that's a penny a
      head.'

But Ted wasn't standing for none o' that there,
    And making an obstinate lip,
'Per tuppence per person per trip,' Ted replied,
    'Per trip or per part of per trip.'

'All right then,' said Father,
    'Let me tak' the boat and I'll pick up the others
      half-way,
I'll row them across and I'll bring the boat back
    And thrupence in t'bargain I'll pay.'

'Twere money for nothing, Ted answered 'Right-o,'
    And Father got 'old of the sculls.
With the sharp end o' boat t'wards middle of stream
    'E were there in a couple of pulls.

'E got Mother out – it were rather a job –
    With the water she weighed 'alf-a-ton;
Then pushing the oar down the side of the boat
    Started fishing around for his son.

When poor little Albert came up to the top
    'Is collar was soggy and limp,

And with 'olding 'is breath at the bottom so long
   'Is face were as red as a shrimp.

Pa took them across and 'e brought the boat back,
   And 'e said to old Ted on the slip,
'Wilt row me across by myself?'
   Ted said 'Aye! at per tuppence per person per trip.'

When they got t'other side Father laughed fit to bust,
   'E'd got best of bargain, y'see,
'E'd worked it all out and 'e'd got 'is own way and
   'E'd paid nobbut fivepence for three.

THE JUBILEE SOV'RIN
By Marriott Edgar (1937)

On Jubilee Day the Ramsbottoms
   Asked all their relations to tea,
Including young Albert's Grandmother –
   An awkward old party were she.

She'd seen Queen Victoria's Jub'lee
   And her weddin' to Albert the Good,
And got quite upset when young Albert
   Asked how she'd got on in the Flood.

She cast quite a damper on t' party,
   But cheered up a bit after tea
And gave Albert a real golden sov'rin
   She'd saved since the last Jubilee.

It had picture of t' Queen on t' one side
   And a dragon fight on the reverse;
It tasted of camphor and cobwebs
   Through being so long in her purse.

Albert cuddled the coin and he kissed it,
   And felt the rough edge with his tongue,
For he knew by the look of his father
   It wouldn't be his very long.

'Shall I get you your money-box, Albert?'
  Said Mother so coaxing and sweet,
And Albert let drop an expression
  He must have picked up in the street.

'I'll show you a trick with that sov'rin,'
  Said Pa, who were hovering near;
Then he took and pretended to eat it
  And brought it back out of his ear.

This magic filled Albert wi' wonder,
  And before you could say 'Uncle Dick'
He'd got the coin back from his father
  And performed the first part of the trick.

When they saw as he'd swallered his sov'rin
  With excitement his relatives burned,
And each one suggested some process
  For getting the money returned.

Some were for fishing with tweezers,
  Some were for shaking it out;
If they only got back a few shillings
  They said 'twould be better than nowt.

They tried holding Albert head downwards,
  And giving his back a good thump;
Then his Uncle, who worked for a chemist,
  Said 'There's nowt for it but stummick pump.'

They hadn't a stummick pump 'andy,
  But Pa did the best that he could
With a bicycle pump as he'd borrowed,
  But that weren't a ha'porth of good.

At the finish they sent for the Doctor,
  Who looked down his throat through glass,
And said 'Aye, this'll mean operation,
  I'm afraid as he'll have to have gas.'

'How much is this 'ere going to cost us?'
  Said Father, beginning to squirm;

Said the Doctor 'It comes quite expensive,
    The gas will be eightpence a therm.'

'Then there's my time, four shillings an hour,
    You can't do these things in two ticks;
By rights I should charge you a guinea,
    But I'll do it for eighteen and six.'

'What, eighteen and six to get sov'rin?'
    Said Father; 'That doesn't sound sense.
I'll tell you what, you'd best keep Albert
    And give me the odd eighteen-pence.'

The Doctor concurred this arrangement
    And to this day remains in some doubt
As to whether he's in eighteen shillings
    Or whether he's eighteen-pence out.

ALBERT AND THE 'EADSMAN
by Marriott Edgar (1937)

On young Albert Ramsbottom's birthday
    His parents asked what he'd like most;
He said to see t' Tower of London
    And gaze upon Anne Boleyn's Ghost.

They thowt this request were unusual,
    And at first to refuse were inclined,
Till Pa said a trip to t' metrollops
    Might broaden the little lad's mind.

They took charrybank up to London
    And got there at quarter to fower,
Then seeing as pubs wasn't open
    They went straight away to the Tower.

They didn't think much to the building,
    'T weren't what they'd been led to suppose,
And the 'Bad Word' Tower didn't impress them,
    They said Blackpool had got one of those.

39

At last Albert found a Beefeater,
    And filled the old chap with alarm
By asking for Ghost of Anne Boleyn,
    As carried her head 'neath her arm.

Said Beefeater 'You ought to come Fridays
    If it's ghost of Anne Boleyn you seek,
Her Union now limits her output,
    And she only gets one walk a week.'

'But,' he said, 'if it's ghosts that you're after,
    There's Lady Jane Grey's to be seen,
She runs around chased by the 'Eadsman
    At midnight on th' old Tower Green.'

They waited on t' green till near midnight,
    Then thinking they'd time for a sup,
They took out what food they'd brought with them
    And waited for t' ghost to turn up.

On the first stroke of twelve, up jumped Albert,
    His mouth full of cold dripping toast,
With his stick with the 'orse's 'ead 'andle
    He pointed, and said ''Ere's the Ghost!'

They felt their skins going all goosey
    As Lady Jane's Spectre drew near,
And Albert fair swallered his tonsils
    When the 'Eadsman an' all did appear.

The 'Eadsman chased Jane round the grass patch,
    They saw his axe flash in the moon,
And seeing as poor lass were headless
    They wondered what next he would prune.

He suddenly caught sight of Albert,
    As midnight was on its last chime;
As he lifted his axe Father murmured
    'We'll get the insurance this time.'

At that Mother rose, taking umbridge;
    She said 'Put that cleaver away.

You're not cutting our Albert's 'ead off,
    Yon collar were clean on to-day.'

The brave little lad stood undaunted
    Till the Ghost were within half a pace,
Then taking the toast he were eating,
    Slapped it, dripping side down, in his face.

'Twere a proper set-back for the 'Eadsman;
    He let out one howl of despair,
Then taking his lady friend with him
    He disappeared – just like that there.

When Pa saw the way as they vanished,
    He trembled with fear and looked blue,
Till Ma went and patted his shoulder
    An' said ''Sallright, lad, we saw it too.'

Some say 'twere the drippin' as done it,
    From a roast leg of mutton it came,
And as th' 'Eadsman had been a Beefeater
    They reckoned he vanished from shame.

And around Tower Green from that moment,
    They've ne'er seen the sign of a ghost,
But when t' Beefeaters go on night duty
    They take slices of cold drippin' toast.

THE RECUMBENT POSTURE

by Marriott Edgar (1939)

The day after Christmas, Young Albert
    Were what's called confined to his bed
With a tight kind of pain in his stummick
    And a light feeling up in his head.

His parents were all of a fluster
    When they saw little lad were so sick;
They said 'Put out your tongue!' – When they'd seen it
    They said 'Put it back again – quick!'

Ma made him a basin of gruel,
    But that were a move for the worse;
Though the little lad tried hard to eat it,
    At the finish he did the reverse.

The pain showed no signs of abating,
    So at last they got Doctor to call;
He said it were in the ab-domain
    And not in his stummick at all.

He sent up a bottle of physick,
    With instructions on t' label to say
'To be took in a recumbent posture,
    One teaspoonful, three times a day.'

As Ma stood there reading the label
    Pa started to fidget about;
He said 'Get a teaspoon and dose him
    Before he gets better without.'

'I can manage the teaspoon,' said Mother,
    A look of distress on her face;
'It's this 'ere recumbulent posture –
    I haven't got one in the place.'

Said Pa 'What about Mrs Lupton
    Next door 'ere – you'd better ask her;
A woman who's buried three husbands
    Is sure to have one of them there.'

So they went round and asked Mrs Lupton.
    'Aye, I know what you mean,' she replied,
'I had got one on order for 'Orace,
    But poor dear got impatient and died.'

She said 'You'd best try the Co-op Shop,
    They'll have one in stock I dare say;
'Fact I think I saw one in the winder
    Last time I were passing that way.'

So round they went to the Co-op Shop,
    And at the counter for household supplies

Pa asked for a recumbent posture,
    And the Shopman said, 'Yes, sir – what size?'

Said Ma 'It's for our little Albert,
    I don't know what size he would use;
I know he takes thirteens in collars,
    And sixes, four fittings, in shoes.'

'If it's little lad's size as you're wanting,'
    Said the Shopman, 'I'm sorry to say
We nobbut had one in the building,
    And that one were sold yesterday.'

He sent them across to a Tin-Smith,
    Who said 'I know what you've in mind;
If you'll draw me a pattern I'll make one' –
    But Pa'd left his pencil behind.

They tried every shop they could think on,
    They walked for two hours by the clock,
And though most places reckoned to keep them,
    They'd none of them got one in stock.

The last place they tried was a Chemist's,
    He looked at them both with a frown,
And told them a Recumbent Posture
    Were Latin, and meant lying down.

'It means 'Lying down' – put in Latin,'
    Said Father, 'That's just what I thowt.'
Then he picked up a side-glance from Mother
    And pretended he hadn't said nowt.

'They're not dosing my lad wi' Latin,'
    Said Mother, her face looking grim;
'Just plain Castor Oil's all he's gettin',
    And I'm leaving the posture to him.'

ALBERT EVACUATED

by Stanley Holloway (1940)

Have you heard how young Albert Ramsbottom
Was evacuated from home
With his mother, clean socks and a toothbrush,
Some Syrup of Figs and a comb.

The stick with the 'orse's 'ead 'andle,
They decided that they'd leave behind
To keep safe with the things they weren't wanting,
Like their gasmasks, and things of that kind.

Pa saw them off at the station,
And shed a few crocodile's tears
As he waved them goodbye from the platform –
T'was the best break he'd had in ten years.

Ma got corner seat for young Albert,
Who amused all the rest of the team
By breathing hot breaths on the window,
And writing some swear words in steam.

They arrived at last somewhere in England,
And straight to their billet were shown;
There was one room for mother
But Albert was in a small room of his own.

The very first night in the blackout,
Young Albert performed quite a feat
By hanging head first from the window,
And shining his torch down the street.

It flashed on an A.R.P. warden
Patrolling with leisurely gait;
'Good Heavens,' said he, 'it's Tarzan,
I'd better go investigate.'

So reading his book of instructions
To make himself doubly sure,

Then in an official ma-nner
Proceeded to knock on the door.

It was opened by Mrs Ramsbottom
'Now then,' said she, 'what's to do?'
And in stern air-warden manner, he said
'I'm going to interrogate you.'

This fair upset Mrs Ramsbottom,
Her face was a picture to see;
'I'll have you know you'll do nowt of the sort,
I'm a respectable woman,' said she.

'Has your son been evacuated?'
Said the A.R.P. man at the door.
'He'd all them things done as a baby,' said Mother
'He's not being done any more.

'Be off, now,' said Mrs Ramsbottom
As she bustled him out of the porch;
And the A.R.P. man patted Albert,
And then confiscated his torch.

Now that were unlucky for Albert,
He had no torch to see him to bed;
But being a bright little fellow
He switched on the hall light instead.

'Put out that light,' a voice shouted.
'Where's the men of our A.R.P.?'
'I've told them already,' the warden replied,
'They take no bloody notice of me.'

Soon Mrs Ramsbottom and Albert
Were feeling quite homesick and sad;
So they thanked the landlady most kindly,
And prepared to go back home to Dad.

When at last they reached home to Father
They were fed up and had quite enough;
But in the front parlour they found six young women,
And Father were doing his stuff.

'Hello, Mother,' said Mr Ramsbottom,
'Come right on in, don't be afraid,
When you went away I joined Ambulance Corps –
I'm instructing the girls in first aid.'

'First aid,' said Mrs Ramsbottom
With a horrible look on her brow.
'If ever you wanted first aid in your life,
By gum, you'll be wanting it now.'

ALBERT'S REUNION
by Stanley Holloway (1978)

You've heard of Albert Ramsbottom,
And Mrs Ramsbottom and Dad,
And the trouble the poor Lion went to
Trying to stomach the lad.

Now after the Lion disgorged him,
Quite many a day had gone by;
But the Lion just sat there and brooded
With a far away look in his eye.

The Keepers could nowt do with Lion
He seemed to be suffering pain,
He seemed to be fretting for summat,
And the curl went out of his mane.

He looked at his food and ignored it,
Just gazed far away into space;
When Keepers tried forcible feeding
They got it all back in their face.

And at Mr and Mrs Ramsbottom's
The same kind of thing had begun –
And though they tried all sorts of measures,
They couldn't rouse Albert their son.

47

Now Mr Ramsbottom got fed up
With trying to please him in vain,
And said 'If you don't start to buck up
I'll take you to Lion again.'

Now instead of the lad getting frightened
And starting to quake at the knees,
He seemed to be highly delighted
And shouted 'Oh, Dad, if you please.'

His father thought he had gone potty,
His Mother went nearly insane,
But Albert just stood there and bellowed
'I want to see Lion again.'

Now Mr and Mrs Ramsbottom
Decided the best thing to do,
Was to give way to Albert
And take him straightaway back to the Zoo.

The moment the Lion saw Albert,
T'were the first time for weeks it had stirred:
It moved the left side of its whiskers,
Then lay on its back and just purred.

And before anybody could stop him,
Young Albert were stroking its paws;
And whilst the crowd screamed for the Keepers
The little lad opened its jaws.

The crowd by this time were dumbfounded,
His Mother was out to the wide,
But they knew by the bumps and the bulges
That Albert were once more inside.

Then all of a sudden the Lion
Stood up and let out a roar;
And Albert, all smiling and happy,
Came out with a thud on the floor.

The crowd by this time were all cheering,
And Albert stood there looking grand

With his stick with the 'orse's 'ead 'andle
Clutched in his chubby young hand.

The Lion grew so fond of Albert
He couldn't be parted from lad;
And so the Zoological Keepers
Sent round a note to his Dad.

'We regret to say Lion is worried
And pining for your little man,
So sending you Lion tomorrow,
Arriving in plain covered van.'

And if you call round any evening,
I'll tell you just what you will see –
Albert is reading to Lion in bed.
And what is he reading? BORN FREE.

PART THREE

Miscellaneous Monologues

THREE HA'PENCE A FOOT
by Marriott Edgar (1932)

I'll tell you an old-fashioned story
　　That Grandfather used to relate,
Of a joiner and building contractor;
　　'Is name, it were Sam Oglethwaite.

In a shop on the banks of the Irwell,
　　Old Sam used to follow 'is trade,
In a place you'll have 'eard of, called Bury;
　　You know, where black puddings is made.

One day, Sam were filling a knot 'ole
　　Wi' putty, when in thro' the door
Came an old feller fair wreathed i' whiskers;
　　T'ould chap said 'Good morning, I'm Noah.'

Sam asked Noah what was 'is business,
　　And t'ould chap went on to remark,
That not liking the look of the weather,
　　'E were thinking of building an Ark.

'E'd gotten the wood for the bulwarks,
　　And all t'other shipbuilding junk,
And wanted some nice Bird's Eye Maple
　　To panel the side of 'is bunk.

Now Maple were Sam's Mon-o-po-ly;
    That means it were all 'is to cut,
And nobody else 'adn't got none;
    So 'e asked Noah three ha'pence a foot.

'A ha'pence too much,' replied Noah,
    'Penny a foot's more the mark;
A penny a foot, and when rain comes,
    I'll give you a ride in me Ark.'

But neither would budge in the bargain;
    The whole daft thing were kind of a jam,
So Sam put 'is tongue out at Noah,
    And Noah made 'Long Bacon' at Sam.

In wrath and ill-feeling they parted,
    Not knowing when they'd meet again,
And Sam had forgot all about it,
    'Til one day it started to rain.

It rained and it rained for a fortni't,
    And flooded the 'ole countryside.
It rained and it kep' on raining,
    'Til the Irwell were fifty miles wide.

The 'ouses were soon under water,
    And folks to the roof 'ad to climb.
They said 'twas the rottonest summer
    That Bury 'ad 'ad for some time.

The rain showed no sign of abating,
    And water rose hour by hour,
'Til the only dry land were at Blackpool,
    And that were on top of the Tower.

So Sam started swimming to Blackpool;
    It took 'im best part of a week.
'Is clothes were wet through when 'e got there,
    And 'is boots were beginning to leak.

'E stood to 'is watch-chain in water,
    On Tower top, just before dark,

When who should come sailing towards 'im
　　But old Noah, steering 'is Ark.

They stared at each other in silence,
　　'Til Ark were alongside, all but,
Then Noah said: 'What price yer Maple?'
　　Sam answered: 'Three ha'pence a foot.'

Noah said 'Nay; I'll make thee an offer,
　　The same as I did t'other day.
A penny a foot and a free ride.
　　Now, come on, lad, what does tha' say?'

'Three ha'pence a foot,' came the answer.
　　So Noah 'is sail 'ad to hoist,
And sailed off again in a dudgeon,
　　While Sam stood determined, but moist.

Noah cruised around, flying 'is pigeons,
　　'Til fortieth day of the wet,
And on 'is way back, passing Blackpool,
　　'E saw old Sam standing there yet.

'Is chin just stuck out of the water;
　　A comical figure 'e cut.
Noah said: '*Now* what's the price of yer Maple?'
　　Sam answered: 'Three ha'pence a foot.'

Said Noah: 'Ye'd best take my offer;
　　It's last time I'll be hereabout;
And if water comes half an inch higher,
　　I'll happen get Maple for nought.'

'Three ha'pence a foot it'll cost yer,
　　And as fer me,' Sam said, 'don't fret.
The sky's took a turn since this morning;
　　I think it'll brighten up yet.'

MANY HAPPY RETURNS

by Archie de Bear (1933)

Down at the school house at Runcorn,
The 'eadmaster walked in one day
Looking all 'appy and cheerful,
Which wasn't his habit, they say.

The boys were completely dumbfounded,
And whispered 'Hello, what's to do?'
But the headmaster still went on smiling
And said, 'Boys, I've some good news for you.'

'It's like this. Today is my birthday,
So it's no time for classes and such –
You can go,' but the boys were too staggered
To even say 'Thanks very much.'

They could scarcely believe their own earholes
As they welcomed these tidings so bright;
But soon they all cheered to the echo,
And very near busted with delight.

Said headmaster 'Now there's no hurry,
Before very long you'll be free;
But seeing as how it's me birthday,
How old would you take me to be?'

Well, the boys didn't like this delaying,
And one of the younger ones swore
At the silly old fool of a master,
And the satisfied smile that he wore.

He didn't swear any too loudly,
Or he'd have been out on the mat
For calling the master a silly old beggar –
Or something that sounded like that.

'I bet you won't guess it correctly,'
The headmaster went on with a wink,

''Cos I've got a sort of a notion
I'm not quite as old as you think.'

A new boy jumped up and guessed twenty,
In the hopes that he'd get off for a week;
While another one guessed ninety-seven –
Although with his tongue in his cheek.

Said the headmaster 'Don't let's be funny,
Or you'll be here all day I can see;
So who'll give a serious guess now,
Come on, just between you and me.'

Then in walked the junior tutor,
In a very old mortar board hat.
He said 'I hear there's a game on,
Well, I'd like a baisin of that.'

Said the headmaster 'Mind your own business,
And kindly do not interfere –
Or you'll lose half your rasher of bacon,
And all your allowance of beer.'

The tutor said 'Don't be a cad, Sir,
I don't wish to make any noise;
But you might at least try to be sporting,
If only in front of the boys.'

With that he swep' out of the classroom,
Fearing the look that he saw –
For he knew that in less than two seconds,
He'd get such a sock in the jaw.

Then in came the language professor,
French teaching was one of his jobs,
So he bowed to the Head and said '*Bonjour,*'
And the Head said '*Bonjour, avec* knobs.'

'But if you've come here to give lessons,
You can take it from me – it's no *bon*
Because today's a holiday. Savvy?
So you might as well *allez-vous en.*'

Then a small voice called 'Sir, why it's easy,
Forty-four is your age I should say.'
Said the master 'Now what a remarkable thing,
You've guessed my right age to the day.'

Said the boy 'Well my brother is just twenty-two.'
Said the headmaster 'What's that to me?'
'Well, Sir, if he's twenty-two you must be forty-four,
'Cos he's only half barmy – see.'

Then the whole class joined in the school anthem,
Which nobody wanted to shirk:
'For he's a jolly good fellow,
So long as we don't have to work.'

GUNNER JOE

by Marriott Edgar (1933)

I'll tell you a seafaring story,
   Of a lad who won honour and fame
Wi' Nelson at Battle Trafalgar –
   Joe Moggeridge, that were his name.

He were one of the crew of the Victory,
   His job when a battle begun
Was to take cannon balls out o' basket
   And shove 'em down front end o' gun.

One day him and Nelson were boxing –
   The compass, like sailor lads do,
When 'Ardy comes up wi' a spyglass
   And pointing, says "'Ere, take a screw!'

They looked to where 'Ardy were pointing
   And saw lots o' ships in a row.
Joe says abrupt-like but respectful,
   "'Oratio lad, yon's the foe.'

57

'What say we attack 'em?' says Nelson,
    Says Joe 'Nay, lad, not to-day,'
And 'Ardy says, 'Aye! well, let's toss up,'
    'Oratio answers 'Okay.'

They tossed – it were heads for attacking
    And tails for t'other way 'bout.
Joe lent them 'is two-headed penny,
    So the answer was never in doubt.

When penny came down 'ead side uppards,
    They was in for a do it were plain,
And Joe murmur'd 'Shiver my timbers,'
    And Nelson kiss'd 'Ardy again.

And then, taking flags out o' locker,
    'E strung out a message on high;
'T were all about England and duty —
    Crew thought they was 'ung out to dry.

They got the guns ready for action,
    And that gave 'em trouble enough,
They 'adn't been fired all the summer
    And touch-holes were bunged up wi' fluff.

Joe's cannon it weren't 'alf a corker,
    The cannon balls went three foot round,
They wasn't no toy balloons neither,
    They weigh'd close on sixty-five pound.

Joe, selecting two of the largest,
    Was going to load double for luck –
When a hot shot came in thro' the porthole
    And a gunpowder barrel got struck.

By gum! there weren't 'alf an explosion,
    The gun crew was filled wi' alarm
As out of the port-hole went Joseph
    Wi' a cannon ball under each arm.

At that moment up came the 'Boat-swine',
    He says 'Where's Joe?'

Gunner replied ''E's taken two cannon balls with 'im
  And gone for a breather outside.'

'Do y'think he'll be long?' says the 'Boat-swine',
  The gunner replied 'If as 'ow
'E comes back as quick as 'e left us,
  'E should be 'ere any time now.'

And all this time Joe, treading water,
  Was trying 'is 'ardest to float,
'E shouted thro' turmoil of battle –
  'Tell someone to lower a boat.'

'E'd come to the top for assistance,
  Then down to the bottom 'e'd go;
This up and down kind of existence
  Made ev'ryone laugh except Joe.

At last 'e could stand it no longer,
  And next time 'e came to the top
'E said 'If you don't come and save me
  I'll let these 'ere cannon balls drop.'

'T were Nelson at finish who saved him
  And 'e said Joe deserved the V.C.,
But finding 'e 'adn't one 'andy
  'E gave Joe an egg for 'is tea.

And after the battle was over,
  And vessel was safely in dock,
The sailors all saved up their coupons
  And bought Joe a nice marble clock.

ATISHOO!

WTH HER HEAD TUCKED UNDERNEATH HER ARM

by R.P. Weston and Bert Lee (1934)

In the Tower of London, large as life
The ghost of Ann Boleyn walks, they declare.
Poor Ann Boleyn was once King Henry's wife –
Until he made the Headsman bob her hair!
Ah yes! he did her wrong long years ago
And she comes up at night to tell him so.

With her head tucked underneath her arm
She walks the Bloody Tower!
With her head tucked underneath her arm
At the Midnight hour –
She comes to haunt King Henry,
She means giving him 'what for',
Gad Zooks, she's going to tell him off for having split her gore.
And just in case the Headsman wants to give her an encore
She has her head tucked underneath her arm!

With her head tucked underneath her arm
She walks the Bloody Tower!
With her head tucked underneath her arm
At the Midnight hour.
Along the draughty corridors for miles and miles she goes,
She often catches cold, poor thing, it's cold there when it blows,
And it's awfully awkward for the Queen to have to blow her nose
With her head tucked underneath her arm!

Sometimes gay King Henry gives a spread
For all his pals and gals – a ghostly crew.
The headsman carves the joint and cuts the bread,
Then in comes Ann Boleyn to 'queer' the 'do';
She holds her head up with a wild war whoop,
And Henry cries 'Don't drop it in the soup!'

With her head tucked underneath her arm
She walks the Bloody Tower!
With her head tucked underneath her arm

At the Midnight hour.
The sentries think that it's a football that she carries in,
And when they've had a few they shout 'Is Ars'nal going to win?'
They think it's Alec James, instead of poor old Ann Boleyn
With her head tucked underneath her arm!

With her head tucked underneath her arm
She walks the Bloody Tower!
With her head tucked underneath her arm
At the Midnight hour.
One night she caught King Henry, he was in the Canteen Bar,
Said he 'Are you Jane Seymour, Ann Boleyn or Cath'rine Parr?
For how the sweet san fairy ann do I know who you are
With your head tucked underneath your arm!'

THE BEEFEATER

by R.P. Weston and Bert Lee (1934)

Introductory Narrative

Oh dear, starting another day I suppose
Showing these 'ere gumps round the Tower.
Still, it's got to be done,
Someone's got to do it.

Good Morning! What's that?
Will I show you round t'Tower, Sir?
You're from Yorkshire, Sir?
Ba goom! The world's small.

I'm from Yorkshire meself – aye;
These 'ere Cockneys don't know
There's a Tower here at all.
First of all, Sir, we come to the canteen

Where you wash the cobwebs off your chest.
That's our motto there –
'Honi soit qui may y pense',
And in Yorkshire that means beer is best.

Monologue

Eh? I'll have a pint, Sir, and thank yer,
You'll find it good ale here to sup.
Well, as Guy Fawkes said when he got bunged in dungeon
And tumbled head first – Bottoms up!

That big 'ole outside is the moat, Sir,
And they do say if ever John Bull
Sells the Tower for a road house with cracks puttied up –
It'll make a damn fine swimming pool.

And now, Sir, we come to armoury;
Here's the tin pants of Dick Coeur de Lion.
Just imagine the job that his old woman had
Putting patches on with soldering iron.

Here's the shirt and chainmail Black Prince wore –
To starch and iron that were real tricky:
It took three boilermakers to put on his shirt,
And a blacksmith to put on his dicky.

And this 'ere's the real headsman's block, Sir,
From this many 'eads fell with a thud –
Ee! To keep these 'ere stains fresh all these three hundred years
We've used buckets and buckets of blood.

'Ere's the axe – that's the genuine axe, Sir,
That's given Royal necks some 'ard whacks.
Tho' it's 'ad a new 'andle and perhaps a new head
But it's a real old original axe.

And down here's where Princes were murdered,
Aye, strangled poor kids in cold blood.
And what's worse, down here I tossed Scotsman for
    shilling –
I won, but the shilling was dud.

And here's where they tortured the prisoners –
On that rack when they wouldn't confess
They were crushed till their life's blood ran drip, drip, drip.
Feeling faint, Sir? Well, here's sergeant's mess.

Eh? Oh, thank you. I will have a pint, Sir,
For talking's a day's work. Bet your life!
For when I show you ducking stool they had for women
By Goom, you'll wish you'd brought the wife.

And why do they call us Beefeaters?
Is it 'cos we eat beef, Sir? Nay, nay.
The Sergeant eats pork and the Corporal eats bacon,
But I eat tripe three times a day.

And so you shall know we're Beefeaters;
There's me who has fought in the wars
'As to walk round with frills on me neck like a hambone,
A daft hat and purple plus fours.

But here's why they call us Beafeaters,
King Alfred, one night so they say
Fell over the feet of the sentry
And shouted Oi! Keep your B-feet out of the way!

ST GEORGE AND THE DRAGON
by R. P. Weston and Bert Lee (1935)

Some folks'll boast about their family trees,
And there's some trees they ought to lop;
But our family tree, believe me, goes right back,
You can see monkeys sitting on top!

To give you some idea of our family tree,
And don't think I'm boastin' nor braggin',
My great, great, great, great, great, great, great Uncle George,
Wor the Saint George who slaughtered the Dragon.

Aye, he wor a blacksmith, not one of the sort
Who shoe horses and sing anvil chorusses,
He used to shoe Dinasauss – big woolly Elephants,
Thumping great Brontosauruses.

Well, one day while he shod a Brontosauruses,
A feller ran into the forge,

He wor shivering with fright and his face pale and white,
And when he got his breath he said 'George –

'Eh, I've just seen a dragon, a whopping great dragon,'
And uncle said 'Seen what? A dragon!
Thou'd best see a doctor, you've got 'em owld lad,
Eh, I thought you were on water wagon!'

But the fellow said, 'Nay, 'twere a big fiery dragon,
'Twere belchin' out fire as it run!'
And Uncle George said 'I could do with a dragon
With coal now at two quid a ton.'

And the feller said 'Eh, but what's more
I've just heard that the old Baron up at the Castle
Says, him as kills Dragon can marry his daughter,
She's lovely and she's worth a parcel.'

Then fellow goes off and old Uncle George thinks,
Of the brass and the bride in old satin,
So he brings out his pup and a pair of his ferrets,
And says to 'em 'We're going ratting.'

The ferrets they cocked up their noses with joy,
And the old Bull pup's tail kept a-waggin',
Then Uncle George shoves 'em a'side rabbit hole,
And says to 'em 'Go on, fetch Dragon.'

Then suddenly he smells a sulphery smell,
Then he sees a big gigantic lizzard,
With smoke coming out of its eyes and its ear'oles,
And flames coming out of its gizzard.

And was George afraid? Yes, he was and he run,
And he hid there in one of the ditches,
While the Dragon, the pig, ate his ferrets and pup,
Aye, best of his prize-winning er – she dogs.

Then George said 'Gad zooks! I'll split thee to the wizzen,
By Gum, but he *were* in a fury,
And he runs to a junk shop, and buys a spear,
And he pinches a Drayhourse from Brew'ry.

Then he sallies forth with a teatray on chest,
On his head he'd a big copper kettle,
With a couple of flat irons to throw at the Dragon,
Owd George were a real man of mettle!

At last he meets Dragon beside of the pump,
Dragon sees him and breathes fire and slaughter,
But George he were ready and in Dragon's mouth,
He just throws a big pail of water!

The Dragon's breath sizzled he'd put out the fire,
Our family are all clever fellows!
Then so as that owd Dragon can't blow up more fire,
With his big spear he punctures his bellows.

Then finding he'd killed it he out with his knife,
He had gumption beside other merits —
And he cuts open Dragon, and under it's vest,
Safe and sound are the pup and the ferrets.

That night the Old Baron gave Uncle his bride,
When he saw her he fainted with horror,
She'd a face like a kite, worse than that the old Baron
Said 'George, you'll be Saint George tomorrow.'

'Course, as St George t'were no drinking nor smoking,
They barred him horse racing as well,
And poor old St George, when he looked at his Bride,
Used to wish that old Dragon to . . . Blazes!

And he got so fed up with this being a Saint,
And the Princess he'd won always naggin',
That he bunked off one day and he opened a pub,
And he called it the 'George and the Dragon'.

And he did a fine trade, eh, for years and for years.
People all came from near and from far there
Just to see Uncle George and the Dragon which he had had,
Stuffed and hung up in the bar there.

T'were a thousand feet long and three hundred feet wide,
But one day while a big crowd observed it,

It fell off the nail, and squashed Uncle George,
And the blinking old liar deserved it.

THE 'OLE IN THE ARK
by Marriott Edgar (1937)

One evening at dusk as Noah stood on his Ark,
   Putting green oil in starboard side lamp,
His wife came along and said – 'Noah, summat's wrong;
   Our cabin is getting quite damp.'

Noah said – 'Is that so?' Then he went down below
   And found it were right what she'd said,
For there on the floor quite a puddle he saw –
   It was slopping around under t' bed.

Said he – 'There's an 'ole in the bottom somewhere,
   We must find it before we retire.'
Then he thowt for a bit, and he said – 'Aye, that's it,
   A bloodhound is what we require.'

So he went and fetched bloodhound from place where it
     lay –
   'Tween the skunk and the polecat it were –
And as things there below were a trifle so-so
   It were glad of a breath of fresh air.

They followed the hound as it went sniffing round,
   Till at last they located the leak;
'Twere a small hole in t' side – about two inches wide,
   Where a sword-fish had poked in its beak.

And by gum! how the wet squirted in through that hole;
   Well, young Shem, who at sums was expert,
Worked it out on his slate that it came at the rate
   Of per gallon, per second, per squirt.

The bloodhound tried hard to keep water in check
   By lapping it up with his tongue,
But it came in so fast through that hole that at last
   He shoved in his nose for a bung.

The poor faithful hound he were very near drowned –
    They dragged him away none too soon,
For the stream as it rose pushed its way up his nose
    And blew him out like a balloon.

And then Mrs Noah shoved her elbow in t' hole
    And said – 'Eeh, it's stopped, I believe.'
But they found very soon as she'd altered her tune,
    For the water had got up her sleeve.

When she saw as her elbow weren't doing much good
    She said to Noah – 'I've an idea:
You sit on the leak, and by t' end of the week
    There's no knowing – weather may clear.'

Noah didn't think much to this notion at all,
    But reckoned he'd give it a try;
On the 'ole down he flopped, and the leaking all stopped,
    And all except him was quite dry.

They took him his breakfast and dinner and tea
    As day after day there he sat,
Till the rain were all passed and they landed at last
    On top side of Mount Ararat.

And that is how Noah got 'em all safe ashore,
    But ever since then, strange to tell,
Them as helped save the Ark has all carried a mark,
    Aye, and all their descendants as well.

That's why dog has a cold nose, and ladies cold elbows –
    You'll also find if you enquire
That that's why a man takes his coat-tails in hand
    And stands with his back to the fire.

JONAH AND THE GRAMPUS

by Marriott Edgar (1937)

I'll tell you the story of Jonah,
   A really remarkable tale;
A peaceful and humdrum existence he had
   Until one day he went for a sail.

The weather were grand when they started,
   But later at turn of the tide
The wind started blowing, the water got rough,
   And Jonah felt funny inside.

When the ship started pitching and tossing
   He tried hard his feelings to smother,
At last he just leant his head over the side
   And one thing seemed to bring up another.

When the sailors saw what he were doing
   It gave them a bit of a jar;
They didn't mind trippers enjoying theirselves,
   But thowt this 'ere were going too far.

Said one 'Is there nowt you can think on
   To stop you from feelin' so bad?'
And Jonah said 'Aye, lift me over the side
   And chuck me in, there's a good lad.'

The Sailor were not one to argue,
   He said 'Happen you know what's best.'
Then he picked Jonah up by the seat of his pants
   And chucked him in, as per request.

A Grampus came up at that moment,
   And seeing the old chap hard set,
It swam to his side and it opened its mouth
   And said 'Come in, lad, out of the wet.'

Its manner were kindly and pleading,
   As if to say 'R.S.V.P.'

Said Jonah 'I've eaten a kipper or two,
    But I never thowt one would eat me.'

The inside of Grampus surprised him,
    'Twere the first time he'd been behind scenes;
He found 'commodation quite ample for one
    But it smelled like a tin of sardines.

Then over the sea they went cruising,
    And Jonah were filled with delight;
With his eye to the blow-'ole in t' Grampus's head
    He watched ships that pass in the night.

'I'm tired of watching,' said Jonah,
    'I'll rest for a minute or so.'
'I'm afraid as you won't find your bed very soft,'
    Said the Grampus – 'I've got a hard roe.'

At that moment up came a whale-boat,
    Said Jonah 'What's this 'ere we've struck?'
'They're after my blubber,' the Grampus replied,
    'You'd better 'old tight while I duck.'

The water came in through the spy-'ole
    And hit Jonah's face a real slosher,
He said 'Shut your blow-'ole!' – and Grampus replied,
    'I can't, lad – it wants a new washer.'

Jo' tried 'ard to bail out the water,
    But found all his efforts in vain,
For as fast as he emptied slops out through the gills
    They came in through the blow-'ole again.

When at finish they came to the surface
    Jo' took a look out and he saw
They were stuck on a bit of a sandbank which lay
    One rod, pole, or perch from the shore.

Said the Grampus 'We're in shallow water,
    I've brought you as far as I may;
If you sit on the blow-'ole on top of my head
    I'll spout you the rest of the way.'

So Jonah obeyed these instructions,
   And the Grampus his lungs did expand,
Then blew out a fountain that lifted Jo' up
   And carried him safely to land.

There was tears in their eyes when they parted
   And each blew a kiss, a real big 'un,
Then t' Grampus went off with a swish of its tail
   And Jonah walked back home to Wigan.

THE PARSON OF PUDDLE
by Greatrex Newman (1975)

In the clean little, green little,
God-save-the-Queen little,
Parish of Puddle o'er which I preside;
There dwells a poor lassie
Who's now rather passé,
There seems to be almost no flesh on her chassis;
And weight-watchers query
And ask for *her* theory,
For she keeps as thin as a *lath* –
And I'm bound to admit
I was shocked quite a bit
When I saw her to-day in her *bath* –
chair, and noticed a skeleton she;
Oh Lack-a-day! Oh Lack-a-day! Oh Lack-a-day *Me!*

In the free little, spree little,
Colour-TV little,
Parish of Puddle o'er which I preside;
We had a school outing
With races and shouting
With little Girls Guiding and little Boys Scouting;
And when all the teachers
Were cooling their features
With bottles they'd bought at an *Inn* –
One said 'Don't you think
You'd like something to drink?'
I said 'Yes, I should love a large *gin* –

ger beer or lemonade, if I may?'
Yea Verily! Yea Verily! Yea Verily! *Yea*!

In the brash little, rash little,
Sausage-and-mash little,
Parish of Puddle o'er which I preside;
It fell to my duty
To wed a blonde beauty
To bridegroom in khaki, a Second Leftootey;
And both were delighted
And got quite excited
When just as a twelve-month had *run* –
One Sunday in May
On a lovely spring day
She presented her spouse with a *Sun* –
day school Hymn Book of Ancient and Mod.;
Odds Bodikins! Odds Bodikins! Odds Bodikins! *Odd*!

In the blank little, swank little,
Two-pubs-and-bank little,
Parish of Puddle o'er which I preside;
A spinster named Mary
Once opened a Dairy,
And as new-laid eggs seemed to be neces*sary* –
She purchased some hens –
Which she fed in their pens,
But when egg-collecting she *went* –
She found with dismay
That those birds could not lay,
For each of those fowls was a *gent* –
(t)*eel* and bashful young rooster, you see;
Oh Fiddle-de! Oh Fiddle-de! Oh Fiddle-de! *Dee*!

In the gay little, stray little,
Hip-hip-Hooray little,
Parish of Puddle o'er which I preside;
A widow – misguided –
Much gossip provided,
And some flk heard more of the details than I did;
So, duty compelling
I called at her dwelling
(I meet all my flock when I *can*) –

As she came to the door
It was plain that she wore
An assortment of beads and a *fan –
tastic* costume she'd bought in Bombay;
Hey Nonny No! Hey Nonny No! Hey Nonny No! *Nay*!

BRAHN BOOTS

by R.P. Weston and Bert Lee (1940)

Our Aunt Hannah's passed away,
We'd her funeral today,
And it was a posh affair –
Had to have two p'licemen there!

The 'earse was luv'ly all plate glass,
And wot a corfin! oak and brass!
We'd fah-sands weepin', flahers gaore,
But Jim, our cousin – what d'yer fink 'e wore?

Why Brahn boots! I ask yer – brahn boots!
Fancy comin' to a funeral in brahn boots!

I will admit 'e 'ad a nice black tie,
Black finger nails and a nice black eye;

But yer can't see people orf when they die in brahn boots!
And Aunt 'ad been so very good to 'im,
Done all that any muvver could fer 'im,
And Jim, her son, to show his clars

Rolls up to make it all a farce
In brahn boots – I ask yer – brahn boots!
While all the rest
Wore decent black and mourning suits.

I'll own he didn't seem so gay,
In fact he cried best part the way,
But straight, he reg'lar spoilt our day
Wiv 'is brahn boots.

In the graveyard we left Jim,
None of us said much to him,
Yus, we all give 'im the bird,
Then by accident we 'eard

'E'd given 'is black boots to Jim Small,
A bloke wot 'ad no boots at all,
So p'raps Aunt Hannah doesn't mind
She did like people who was good and kind.

But brahn boots! I ask yer – brahn boots!
Fancy coming to a funeral in brahn boots!
And we could 'ear the neighbours all remark
'Wot, 'im chief mourner? Wot a bloomin' lark!

'Why 'e looks more like a Bookmaker's clerk – in brahn boots!'
That's why we 'ad to be so rude to 'im,
That's why we never said 'Ow do!' to 'im,
We didn't know – he didn't say.

He'd give 'is other boots away.
But brahn boots! I ask yer – brahn boots!
While all the rest
Wore decent black and mourning suits!

But some day up at Heaven's gate
Poor Jim, all nerves will stand and wait
Till an angel whispers 'Come in, Mate,
Where's yer brahn boots?'

YORKSHIRE PUDDEN!

by R. P. Weston and Bert Lee (1940)

Hi waitress, excuse me a minute, now listen,
I'm not finding fault, but here, Miss,
The 'taters' look gradely – the beef is a' reet
But what kind of pudden is this?

It's what? – Yorkshire pudden!, now coom coom coom coom,
It's what! Yorkshire pudden d'ye say!
It's pudden I'll grant you – it's some sort o' pudden,
But not Yorkshire pudden, nay nay!

The real Yorkshire pudden's a poem in batter,
To make one's an art not a trade,
Now listen to me – for I'm going to tell thee
How t' first Yorkshire pudden wor made.

A young angel on furlough from Heaven
Came flying above Ilkley Moor
And this angel, poor thing – got cramp in her wing
And coom down at auld woman's door.

The ould woman smiled and said 'Ee, it's an angel,
Well I am surprised to see thee,
I've not seen an angel before but thou'rt welcome,
I'll make thee a nice cup o' tea.'

The angel said 'Ee, thank you kindly I will,'
Well she had two or three cups of tea,
Three or four Sally Lunns, and a couple of buns –
Angels eat very lightly you see.

The t'owd woman looking at clock said 'By Gum!
He's due home from mill is my Dan,

75

You get on wi' ye tea, but ye must excuse me,
I must make pudden now for t'owd man.'

Then the angel jumped up and said 'Gimme your bowl –
Flour and t'watter and eggs, salt and all,
And I'll show thee how we make puddens in Heaven,
For Peter and Thomas and Paul.'

Then t'owd woman gave her the things, and the angel
Just pushed back her wings and said 'Hush!'
Then she tenderly tickled the mixture wi' t'spoon
Like an artist would paint with his brush.

Aye, she mixed up that pudden with Heavenly magic,
She played with her spoon on that dough
Just like Paderewski would play the piano
Or Kreisler now deceased would twiddle his bow.

And when it wor done and she put it in t'oven
She said t'owd woman 'Goodbye',
Then she flew away leaving the first Yorkshire pudden
That ever was made – and that's why.

It melts in the mouth, like the snow in the sunshine
As light as a maiden's first kiss;
As soft as the fluff on the breast of a dove
Not elephant's leather like this!

It's real Yorkshire pudden that makes Yorkshire lassies
So buxom and broad in the hips,
It's real Yorkshire pudden that makes Yorkshire cricketers
Win County championships.

It's real Yorkshire pudden that gives me my dreams
Of a real Paradise up above,
Where at the last trump I'll queue up for a lump
Of the real Yorkshire pudden I love!

And there on a cloud – far away from the crowd
In a real Paradise, not a 'dud' 'un,
I'll do nowt for ever and ever and ever
But gollup up real Yorkshire pudden!

UPPARDS

(A Lancashire Version of Longfellow's Famous Poem 'Excelsior')

by Marriott Edgar (1941)

'Twere getting dusk
   One winter's night
When up the clough
   There came in sight
A lad who carried through the snow
A banner with this 'ere motto:
     'Uppards'.

His face was glum
   As he did pass,
His eyes was shiny
   Just like glass,
And as he went upon his way
He nobbut this 'ere word did say:
     'Uppards'.

And people sitting
   Down to tea
They heard him plain
   As plain could be,
They thowt 'twere final football score
As this 'ere word rang out once more:
     'Uppards'.

A P'liceman on
   His lonely beat
He stopped the lad
   Up t' end of t' street.
He said 'Wheer't going wi' that theer?'
The lad just whispered in his ear:
     'Uppards'.

'Don't go down t' clough,'
   The P'liceman said,
'It's mucky road
   For thee to tread,

Canal's at bottom deep and wide.'
'That's not my road,' the lad replied,
     'It's "Uppards".'

A young Lass stopped him
     Further up,
She said 'Come in
     Wi' me and sup.'
He said 'I'm taking none o' yon,
Besides, I must be gettin' on
       "Uppards".'

Next morn some lads
     Had just begun
To tak' their whippets
     For a run
When dogs got scratching in the snow
And found flag with this 'ere motto:
       'Uppards'.

That set them digging
     All around,
And 'twasn't long
     Before they found
A lad whose name they never learned,
Whose face was white, whose toes was turned
       'Uppards'.

'Twere very plain
     For to behold
The lad had ta'en
     His death o' cold;
He'd got his feet wet early on
And from his feet the cold had gone
       'Uppards'.

This story only
     Goes to show
That when the fields
     Is white wi' snow
It's inadvisable to go:
       'Uppards'.

SWEENEY TODD, THE BARBER

by R. P. Weston and Bert Lee (1935)

In Fleet Street that's in London Town,
When King Charlie wore the Crown,
There lived a man of great renown,
It was Sweeney Todd, the Barber.

One shave from him and you'd want no more –
You'd feel his razor sharp
Then tumble wallop through the floor
And wake up playing a harp

– and singing.

Sweeney Todd, the Barber
Ba Goom, he were better than a play,
Sweeney Todd, the Barber
'I'll polish him off,' he used to say.

His clients through the floor would slope,
But he had no fear of the hangman's rope
Dead men can't talk with their mouths full of soap,
Said Sweeney Todd, the Barber.

Now underneath the shop it's true
Where other bodies tumbled through
There lived a little widow who
Loved Sweeney Todd the Barber.

She made her living by selling pies,
Her meat pies were a treat,
Chock full of meat and such a size
'Cos she was getting the meat from

Mr Sweeney Todd, the Barber.
Ba Goom, he were better than a play
Sweeney Todd, the Barber
'I'll polish them off,' he used to say.

And many's the poor young orphan lad
'Ad the first square meal he'd ever had –

A hot meat pie, made out of his Dad
From Sweeney Todd, the Barber.

It was Saturday night in old Sweeney Todd's shop
And his customers sat in a row
While Sweeney behind a screen shaved some poor mug
And his sweetheart made pies down below.

Though none were aware, it were cut prices there
They were rolling up in twos and threes,
And his foot was quite sore pressing knob on the floor
And his voice went from saying 'Next please'.

First a swell took the chair He said Ha, Ha, my man,
He said 'Ha, Ha, my man,
Just a shave and a perfumed shampoo
For I've just got engaged.' Sweeney just pressed the knob
and said 'There now, it's all fallen through.'
    fallen through.'

Then a bookmaker said, with his mouth full of saop,
'They're all backing favourites today
So I'll bet I'll go down.' Sweeney said 'So you will,'
And he did – he went down straight away.

But what rotten luck – the darned trap went and stuck
For the hinge he'd forgotten to grease;
And a customer there started calling out 'Police',
Just as Sweeney was saying 'Next please'.

Yes, he ran to the door and he shouted 'Police',
He called 'Police' nine times or ten;
But no policeman arrived and a very good reason
The police weren't invented by then.

But up came the brave Bow Street runners – hurray!
And he had to let many a pie burn
While they dragged him to quad, And next day Sweeney Todd
Was condemned to be switched off at Tyburn.

And there on the gibbet he hangs in chains,
And they do say a little black crow

Made a sweet little nest In Old Sweeney Todd's whiskers
And sang as he swang to and fro.

Sweeney Todd, the Barber
Ba Goom, he were better than a play;
Sweeney Todd, the Barber
They buried him underneath the clay.

And old Nick calls him from his grave
Shouting 'Wake up, Sweeney, I want a shave,'
And Mrs Nick wants a permanent wave
From, Sweeney Todd, The Barber.

THE BATTLE OF HASTINGS
by Marriott Edgar (1937)

I'll tell of the Battle of Hastings,
   As happened in days long gone by,
When Duke William became King of England,
   And 'Arold got shot in the eye.

It were this way – one day in October
   The Duke, who were always a toff,
Having no battles on at the moment,
   Had given his lads a day off.

They'd all taken boats to go fishing,
   When some chap in t' Conqueror's ear
Said 'Let's go and put breeze up the Saxons;'
   Said Bill – 'By gum, that's an idea.'

Then turning around to his soldiers,
   He lifted his big Norman voice,
Shouting – 'Hands up who's coming to England.'
   That was swank 'cos they hadn't no choice.

They started away about tea-time –
   The sea was so calm and so still,
And at quarter to ten the next morning
   They arrived at a place called Bexhill.

King 'Arold came up as they landed –
　　His face full of venom and 'ate –
He said 'If you've come for Regatta
　　You've got here just six weeks too late.'

At this William rose, cool but 'aughty,
　　And said – 'Give us none of your cheek;
You'd best have your throne re-upholstered,
　　I'll be wanting to use it next week.'

When 'Arold heard this 'ere defiance,
　　With rage he turned purple and blue,
And shouted some rude words in Saxon,
　　To which William answered – 'And you.'

'Twere a beautiful day for a battle;
　　The Normans set off with a will,
And when both sides was duly assembled,
　　They tossed for the top of the hill.

King 'Arold he won the advantage,
　　On the hill-top he took up his stand,
With his knaves and his cads all around him,
　　On his 'orse with his 'awk in his 'and.

The Normans had nowt in their favour,
　　Their chance of a victory seemed small,
For the slope of the field were against them,
　　And the wind in their faces and all.

The kick-off were sharp at two-thirty,
　　And soon as the whistle had went
Both sides started banging each other
　　Till the swineherds could hear them in Kent.

The Saxons had best line of forwards,
　　Well armed both with buckler and sword –
But the Normans had best combination,
　　And when half-time came neither had scored.

So the Duke called his cohorts together
　　And said – 'Let's pretend that we're beat,

Once we get Saxons down on the level
  We'll cut off their means of retreat.'

So they ran – and the Saxons ran after,
  Just exactly as William had planned,
Leaving 'Arold alone on the hill-top
  On his 'orse with his 'awk in his 'and.

When the Conqueror saw what had happened,
  A bow and an arrow he drew;
He went right up to 'Arold and shot him.
  He were off-side, but what could they do?

The Normans turned round in a fury,
  And gave back both parry and thrust,
Till the fight were all over bar shouting,
  And you couldn't see Saxons for dust.

And after the battle were over
  They found 'Arold so stately and grand,
Sitting there with an eye-full of arrow
  On his 'orse with his 'awk in his 'and.

THE MAGNA CHARTER

by Marriott Edgar (1937)

I'll tell of the Magna Charter
  As were signed at the Barons' command
On Runningmead Island in t' middle of t' Thames
  By King John, as were known as 'Lack Land'.

Some say it were wrong of the Barons
  Their will on the King so to thrust,
But you'll see if you look at both sides of the case
  That they had to do something, or bust.

For John, from the moment they crowned him,
  Started acting so cunning and sly,
Being King, of course, he couldn't do any wrong,
  But, by gum, he'd a proper good try.

He squandered the ratepayer's money,
    All their cattle and corn did he take,
'Til there wasn't a morsel of bread in the land,
    And folk had to manage on cake.

The way he behaved to young Arthur
    Went to show as his feelings was bad;
He tried to get Hubert to poke out his eyes,
    Which is no way to treat a young lad.

It were all right him being a tyrant
    To vassals and folks of that class,
But he tried on his tricks with the Barons an' all,
    And that's where he made a faux pass.

He started bombarding their castles,
    And burning them over their head,
'Til there wasn't enough castles left to go round,
    And they had to sleep six in a bed.

So they went to the King in a body,
    And their spokesman, Fitzwalter by name,
He opened the 'ole in his 'elmet and said,
    Concil-latory like, 'What's the game?'

The King starts to shilly and shally,
    He sits and he haws and he hums,
'Til the Barons in rage started gnashing their teeth,
    And them with no teeth gnashed their gums.

Said Fitz, through the 'ole in his 'elmet,
    'It was you as put us in this plight.'
And the King having nothing to say to this 'ere
    Murmured 'Leave your address and I'll write.'

This angered the gallant Fitzwalter;
    He stamped on the floor with his foot,
And were starting to give John a rare ticking off,
    When the 'ole in his 'elmet fell shut.

'We'll get him a Magna Charter,'
    Said Fitz when his face he had freed;

Said the Barons, 'That's right and if one's not enough,
   Get a couple and happen they'll breed.'

So they set about making a Charter,
   When at finish they'd got it drawn up,
It looked like a paper on cattle disease,
   Or the entries for t' Waterloo Cup.

Next day, King John, all unsuspecting,
   And having the afternoon free,
To Runningmead Island had taken a boat,
   And were having some shrimps for his tea.

He had just pulled the 'ead off a big 'un,
   And were pinching its tail with his thumb,
When up came a barge load of Barons, who said,
   'We thought you'd be here so we've come.'

When they told him they'd brought Magna Charter,
   The King seemed to go kind of limp,
But minding his manners he took off his hat
   And said 'Thanks very much, have a shrimp.'

'You'd best sign at once,' said Fitzwalter,
   'If you don't, I'll tell thee for a start
The next coronation will happen quite soon,
   And you won't be there to take part.'

So they spread Charter out on t' tea table,
   And John signed his name like a lamb,
His writing in places was sticky and thick
   Through dipping his pen in the jam.

And it's through that there Magna Charter,
   As were signed by the Barons of old,
That in England to-day we can do what we like,
   So long as we do what we're told.

PART FOUR

Monologue Discography

(*Note:* Unless otherwise indicated, all records listed are the original 78 rpm recordings. Details of Long Playing Records show new recordings and re-issues separately.)

Part I – SAM SMALL

Old Sam (Sam, Pick Oop Tha' Musket) London, 27 October, 1930. Piano accompaniment by Wolseley Charles. Columbia DX-168.
London, 13 May, 1940. Piano accompaniment by Leo Conriche. Columbia FB-2470.
Reissued on EMI-ONCM 515 (33⅓ LP record, London, 1978).

'Alt! Who Goes There? London, 27 October, 1930. Piano accompaniment by Wolseley Charles. Columbia DX-168.
London, 13 May, 1940. Piano accompaniment by Leo Conriche. Columbia FB-2470.
Reissued on EMI-ONCM 515 (33⅓ LP record, London, 1978).

Beat The Retreat on Thy Drum (Sam, Sam, Beat the Retreat) London, 11 December, 1931. Piano accompaniment by Wolseley Charles. Columbia DX-321.
London, 16 May, 1940. Piano accompaniment by Leo Conriche. Columbia FB-2498.
Reissued on EMI-ONCM 515 (33⅓ LP record, London, 1978).

One Each Apiece All Round London, 11 December, 1931. Piano accompaniment by Wolseley Charles. Columbia DX-321.
London, 16 May, 1940. Piano accompaniment by Leo Conriche. Columbia FB-2498.
Reissued on EMI-ONCM 515 (33⅓ LP record, London, 1978).

Sam's Medal London, 9 June, 1933. Piano accompaniment by Wolseley Charles. Columbia DX-474.
Reissued on EMI-ONCM 515 (33⅓ LP record,   London, 1978).

Old Sam's Party London, 13 September, 1933. Piano accompaniment by Wolseley Charles. Columbia DX-512.

Marksman Sam London, 13 November, 1934. Piano accompaniment by Wolseley Charles. Columbia DX-650.
London, 23 August, 1940. Piano accompaniment by Leo Conriche. Columbia FB-2539.
Reissued on EMI-ONCM 515 (33⅓ LP record,   London, 1978).
New version accompanied by Chris Heath. Argo 2DA170 (33⅓ LP record, 1975).

Sam Drummed Out London, 15 November, 1935. Piano accompaniment by Wolseley Charles. Columbia DX-718.
Reissued on EMI-ONCM 515 (33⅓ LP record,   London, 1978).

Sam's Sturgeon London, 15 November, 1935. Piano accompaniment by Wolseley Charles. Columbia DX-718.
Reissued EMI-ONCM 515 (33⅓ LP record,   London, 1978).

Old Sam's Christmas Pudding London, 16 May, 1939. Piano accompaniment by Leo Conriche. Columbia DX-948.

Sam Goes To It London, 9 August, 1941. Piano accompaniment by W. T. Best. Columbia FB-2680.

Part II – ALBERT RAMSBOTTOM

The Lion and Albert London, 16 May, 1932. Piano accompaniment by Wolseley Charles. Columbia DX-353.
London, 13 May, 1940. Piano accompaniment by Leo Conriche. Columbia FB-2482.
Reissued on EMI-ONCM 515 (33⅓ LP record,   London, 1978).

The Return of Albert (Albert Comes Back) London, 13 November, 1934. Piano accompaniment by Wolseley Charles. Columbia DX-650.
London, 23 August, 1940. Piano accompaniment by Leo Conriche. Columbia FB-2482.
Reissued on EMI-ONCM 515 (33⅓ LP record,   London, 1978).

Runcorn Ferry (Tuppence Per Person Per Trip) London, 20 July, 1933. Piano accompaniment by Wolseley Charles. Columbia DX-559.
Reissued on EMI-ONCM 515 (33⅓ LP record,   London, 1978).

The Jubilee Sov'rin London, 10 February, 1937. Piano accompaniment by
Wolseley Charles. Columbia DX-770.
Reissued on EMI-ONCM 515 (33⅓ LP record,   London, 1978).

Albert and the 'Eadsman London, 10 February, 1937. Piano accompaniment
by Wolseley Charles. Columbia DX-770.
Reissued on EMI-ONCM 515 (33⅓ LP record,   London, 1978).

The Recumbent Posture London, 16 May, 1939. Piano accompaniment by
Leo Conriche. Columbia DX-948.
Reissued on Music for Pleasure MFP-1114 (33⅓ LP record,

New version accompanied by Michael Garrick on Argo ZDA-170
(33⅓ LP record, 1975).

Albert Evacuated London, 11 March, 1940. Piano accompaniment by
Leo Conriche. Columbia FB-2408.
Reissued on EMI-ONCM 515 (33⅓ LP record,   London, 1978).

Albert's Reunion London, 1975. Piano accompaniment by Chris Hazell.
Argo ZDA-170. (33⅓ LP record.)

Part III – MISCELLANEOUS MONOLOGUES

Three Ha'pence a Foot London, 16 March, 1932. Piano accompaniment
by Wolseley Charles. Columbia DX-353.
Reissued on Music for Pleasure MFP-1114 (33⅓ LP record,

Many Happy Returns London, 9 June, 1933. Piano accompaniment by
Wolseley Charles. Columbia DX-474.

Gunner Joe London, 20 July, 1933. Piano accompaniment by Wolseley
Charles. Columbia DX-559.
Reissued on Music for Pleasure MFP-1114 (33⅓ LP record,

New version accompanied by Michael Garrick on Argo ZDA-170.
(33⅓ LP record, 1975.)

With Her Head Tucked Underneath Her Arm London, 7 September, 1934.
Piano accompaniment by Wolseley Charles. Columbia DX-603.
Reissued on Music for Pleasure MFP-1114 (33⅓ LP record,

The Beafeater London, 7 September, 1934. Piano accompaniment by
Wolseley Charles. Columbia DX-603.
Reissued on EMI-ONCM 515 (33⅓ LP record,   London, 1978).

St George and the Dragon London, 1975. Piano accompaniment by Chris Hazell. Argo ZDA-170. (33⅓ LP record.)

The 'Ole in the Ark London, 1 December, 1937. Piano accompaniment by Wolseley Charles. Columbia DX-821.
Reissued on EMI-ONCM 515 (33⅓ LP record,   London, 1978).

Jonah and the Grampus London, 1 December, 1937. Piano accompaniment by Wolseley Charles. Columbia DX-821.
Reissued on Music for Pleasure MFP-1114 (33⅓ LP record,

The Parson of Puddle (original version) London, 8 November, 1938. Piano accompaniment by Wolseley Charles. Columbia FB-2093.

New version (in this book) accompanied by Chris Hazell on Argo ZDA-170 (33⅓ LP record, 1975).

Brahn Boots London, 29 October, 1940. Piano accompaniment by Leo Conriche. Columbia FB-2526.
Reissued on EMI-ONCM 515 (33⅓ LP record,   London, 1978).

New version, London, 11 April, 1961. Orchestra conducted by Tony Osborne. Columbia DB-4653 (45 rpm record).

London, 11 April, 1961. Orchestra conducted by Tony Osborne. Columbia DB-4653 (45 rpm record).

Yorkshire Pudden! London, 29 October, 1940. Piano accompaniment by Leo Conriche. Columbia FB-2526.

Uppards London, 9 August, 1941. Piano accompaniment by W. T. Best. Columbia FB-2680.

Sweeney Todd, The Barber New York, 1957. Orchestra conducted by Arthur Liet Phillips BBL-7237 (33⅓ LP record).

The Battle of Hastings London, 1975. Piano accompaniment by Chris Hazell. Argo ZDA-170 (33⅓ LP record).

The Magna Charter London, 1975. Piano accompaniment by Chris Hazell. Argo ZDA-170 (33⅓ LP record).